AMERICA'S
YOUTH
IN
CRISIS

AMERICA'S YOUTH IN CRISIS

Challenges and Options for Programs and Policies

CRISIS

Richard M. Lerner

Sponsored by the National 4-H Council

SAGE Publications
International Educational and Professional Publisher
Thousand Oaks   London   New Delhi

For information address:

 SAGE Publications, Inc.
2455 Teller Road
Thousand Oaks, California 91320

SAGE Publications Ltd.
6 Bonhill Street
London EC2A 4PU
United Kingdom

SAGE Publications India Pvt. Ltd.
M-32 Market
Greater Kailash I
New Delhi 110048 India

Printed in the United States of America

Library of Congress Cataloging-in-Publication Data

Lerner, Richard M.
America's youth in crisis: challenges and options for programs and policies / Richard M. Lerner.
p. cm.
Includes bibliographical references and indexes.
ISBN 0-8039-7068-4 (cl.).—ISBN 0-8039-7069-2 (pbk.)
1. Youth—United States. 2. Youth—Government policy—United States. 3. Education and state—United States. 4. Poverty—United States. I. Title.
HQ796.L382 1995
305.23'5'0973—dc20   94-34626

95 96 97 98 99 10 9 8 7 6 5 4 3 2 1

Sage Production Editor: Yvonne Könneker

Contents

Foreword *by Joy G. Dryfoos*   vii

Foreword *by Richard J. Sauer*   ix

Foreword *by Justin S. Lerner*   xi

Preface   xiii

1. The Contemporary Crises of America's Children and Adolescents   1

    Illustrations of Risk Behaviors   2
    Temporal Trends in Risk Behaviors   6
    Child and Youth Poverty   7
    Addressing the Crisis Through an Integrative Theory of Human Development   11

2. An Overview of Developmental Contextualism   14

    Children's Influences on Their Own Development   17
    Development as a Life-Span Phenomenon   20
    Development in Its Ecological Context   23
    Implications for Research and Application   31

3. An Integrative Vision of Human Development Research and Outreach   33

    A Focus on Diversity   36
    Implications for Policies and Programs   51
    Toward the Creation of an Integrated Agenda   54
    The Role of Applied Developmental Scientists   56

4. Designing Successful Prevention Programs   61

    The Good News and the Bad News
       of Successful Youth Programs   65
    Features of Successful Programs   68
    Conclusions   76

5. Key Principles of Successful Prevention Programs   77

    Building the Capacity of Youth and Families Through
       Collaborative Evaluation Methods   81
    Features of Development-in-Context Evaluations   87
    Developmental Contextualism and Program Design
       and Evaluation   92
    The Potential Role of Programs Involving Community-Wide,
       Integrative Multiagency Collaborations:
       The Sample Case of Full-Service Schools   92
    Conclusions   98

6. Meeting the Challenges Facing America's
   Universities by Integrating Research and Outreach   100

    The American Land-Grant University and the
       Vision of Home Economics   101
    Outreach Scholarship   104
    The Campus Context   105
    The Community Context   110
    Conclusions   115

7. Implications for Social and Academic Policy   117

    Toward the Development of a National Youth Policy   118
    Implications of Developmental Contextualism for
       Youth Policy   122
    Dimensions of Academic Policy Change   126
    Conclusions   127

References   129

Name Index   140

Subject Index   145

About the Author   147

Foreword

You don't need to be a rocket scientist to figure out that all is not well on the home front. Appalling statistics on child and youth welfare portend terrible suffering—daily portraits in the press of homicidal children and homeless, hungry babies translate the numbers into real people. But the general public does not just get up in the morning highly motivated to address social issues. Most are focused on their own welfare, worrying about their own kids, maintaining their own relationships, and keeping their taxes down. They have little insight into how those misery statistics affect the quality of their lives and the lives of generations to come.

Fortunately, within the general population resides a growing body of human resources people, both professionals and volunteers, who want to confront the statistics and the causes behind them and reshape this nation. Richard Lerner is one of those reshapers. I am delighted that he has built on my work and the work of my colleagues to develop an agenda for integrating research and outreach.

Although he generously refers to me as a scholar, I describe myself as an angry old activist. In my view, the purpose of research is to inform action, and the role of the university is to produce practitioners of many varieties who can implement that action. As this book suggests, enough research currently exists to initiate planned responses to the interrelated problems of families, schools, and communities. And if researchers can be lured into program evaluation and operational research, we could move faster and better.

The real test for all of our theories lies out in the field, in the diverse American communities. We know now that human service workers must move away from their concentration on changing individual behaviors and tackle the challenges involved in institutional change. Richard Lerner describes what I call my obsession with full-service schools, the model that combines, in one setting, quality education and support services (everything needed in that community to help children, adolescents, and families "make it"). This concept is based on the premise that neither kind of intervention—educational nor social—will be successful without the other.

In all parts of the country, the consensus is that more comprehensive and powerful programs are required. Communities need help in arriving at that shared vision of new institutional arrangements, technical assistance with putting all the pieces together, and long-term support that will ensure institutionalization of demonstrations and real change in the life chances for children and their families.

We are all in this together. Land-grant universities are in a unique position to bridge the gap between research and practice. The extension service researches into every community in America and has the potential for bringing together local leaders, agencies, parents, youth, and media to shape and act on that vision. This book should guide those endeavors, sensitizing practitioners to respond to critical needs, charging researchers to focus on relevant issues, and challenging universities to integrate curricula and produce real leaders for the future.

JOY G. DRYFOOS

Foreword

Refreshing—even amazing!—to find a distinguished academic scholar who is not content with producing research that meets the scrutiny of peers and is published in the best journals in the field. Rather, his satisfaction must come from seeing his research and that of his colleagues and peers applied in the formation of an agenda and effective action plan for the nation's children and adolescents. If he can lead by example and attract other scholars to risk joining him in applied research, outreach, and evaluation, then we have a legitimate chance of responding in time to a huge and growing crisis in this country—the vast underrealization of the potential of our children and the concurrent growing jeopardy of our nation and society as we have known it.

Richard Lerner understands that our children, adolescents, families, and communities and society are growing in complexity and diversity, due to the confluence of many forces. And he has risked candidly criticizing his profession for having focused its research attention largely on White, middle-class children and adolescents, resulting in a theoretical and a practical knowledge gap between existing data and the needs of the nation's diverse youth and families. If he can capture the attention and engage the talents of his peers, the gap can be closed in time to make use of the data in addressing our crisis.

With comprehensive data, Richard Lerner has demonstrated that "the breadth and depth of the problems besetting our nation's youth, families, and communities exist at historically unprecedented levels." And he has articulated the most effective route to applying ourselves in creative action for the positive development of our children and adolescents. He has identified that we must focus our energies on local communities—engaging the total community to overcome turf barriers and build comprehensive, integrated, sustainable community-based programs.

4-H has supported the publication of this book because it represents a hope for engaging the scholars of academic communities, in land-grant universities and elsewhere, to focus their research on addressing the real-world problems of today's diverse children, adolescents, and families. If they begin to do so, 4-H and other youth development education programs will finally have a relevant body of knowledge undergirding the work they undertake on behalf of children and adolescents.

We must commit ourselves to holistic systems in support of positive youth development at the community level. Richard Lerner articulates the critical need for doing so, the specific, collaborative role academic scholars can play, and the enormous potential societal benefit from giving this our highest priority.

RICHARD J. SAUER
President and CEO
National 4-H Council

Foreword

For about 180 days of the year, roughly 1,125 kids around the town I live in come to school. Each day, every boy and girl of that 1,125 makes decisions. They, including myself, make decisions that, whether they know it or not, affect them. The decisions could affect what happens in a day, week, year, or life.

It's hard for kids my age to relate to what adults write. Either you won't understand it, or you don't want to. That's why, when I was asked to write this foreword, I thought it would be an opportunity to get my perspective and those of many other people's across. So, instead of reading a book about kids written by all adults, the views of a 14-year-old will be consolidated with adults' views.

Even though my school is pretty much safe, there still are drugs, there still is violence, and there still are dropouts (to name a few problems). Peer pressure and acceptance are major forces in these categories. If we were rid of those two forces, dropouts, drugs, and violence would be a problem of dwindling importance.

But in reality, they will always be there. As I said earlier, choices are made every day. Kids choose what group to be categorized with. In my opinion, one of the most important things in my life and the lives of kids my age is being accepted by our peers. It ranks higher on some people's priority list than others. Some people will do things like try drugs or cut class to be accepted. It works. It may sound stupid. It is.

You can also think of it like this. There are two kinds of problems. A short-term problem like "Who should I ask to the dance?" can be resolved by using a short-term solution. A long-term problem can and will affect the rest of your life. They are best resolved with a long-term solution. We screw up when we use a short-term solution for a long-term problem. A long-term problem could be something like deciding to smoke—"Some popular kids are going to the mall; they'll probably like me if they see me smoking; should I do it?" Short-term solution—"If I only do it once they'll like me; I won't do it again; I won't get caught." Before deciding, what you should do is ask yourself, "How will this hurt me in the long run?"

This is only an example of what might occur. Each day, kids in the United States are probably faced with similar decisions. I have taken my school as an example. There are many other schools. Some are much better. A lot are much worse. There are worse situations that I know happen. You can go back to the first thing I said: Each and every kid makes decisions, ones from the simplest thing like, "Should I go to my next class?" to a decision that could affect their life.

Before kids have the responsibility of making their own decisions, we need to know how to judge making them. I hope that this book will help kids deal with these issues.

JUSTIN S. LERNER
Okemos, MI

Preface

Don't children usually grow up healthy and fine? Don't they usually emerge intact from their early "growing pains"? Yes and no. While it is certainly true that many turn out well, with or without great difficulty in mid-passage, it is also true that far too many are experiencing the formidable but preventable burdens of ignorance, illness, suffering, failure, humiliation, and lost opportunities. For instance, the evidence indicates that about one adolescent in four is in really serious trouble, such as pregnancy, drug use, dropping out of school, depression and suicide. We lag well behind the other advanced democracies in preventing infant mortality; during the eighties, twenty nations did better. Measures of educational achievement—in reading, math, and science—reveal that our children badly fail to meet the standards of other technically advanced nations. In short, a variety of indices indicate that we are suffering heavy casualties during the years of growth and development, and these casualties not only are tragic for the individuals but also bear heavy cost for American society.

David A. Hamburg (1992, p. 1)[1]

America is hanging over a precipice. Unless dramatic and innovative action is taken soon, millions of our nation's children and adolescents—the human capital on which America must build its future—will fall into an abyss of crime and violence, drug and alcohol use and abuse, unsafe sex, school failure, lack of job preparedness, and feelings of despair and hopelessness that pervade the lives of children whose parents have lived in poverty and who see themselves as having little opportunity to do better, that is, to have a life marked by societal respect, achievement, and opportunity.

The waste of our children's lives continues, seemingly unabated, each year. Indeed, I believe that the breadth and depth of the problems besetting our nation's youth, families, and communities exist at historically unprecedented levels. Moreover, even if one believes that his or her own children are not engaged directly in high-risk behaviors, and even if one's own family is not poor, few people consider themselves or their children immune from such dangers as random violence; few believe that their communities or businesses can continue to prosper if the economic competitiveness of the American economy rests on cohorts of youth wherein drug and alcohol use and abuse, school failure and dropout, delinquency and crime, and teenage pregnancy and parenting are increasingly more prototypic occurrences. As such, it is not just *some* youth that are at risk, or just *some* communities that face the problems of losing much of their next generation. It is all of America's children, all our children, that are at risk.

The loss of so much of our young generations is needless. There is increasing evidence that effective means exist about how to prevent the actualization of the numerous behavioral risks confronting our nation's youth and many of the sequelae of persistent and pervasive poverty. Scholars and child advocates such as Joy Dryfoos, Lisbeth Schorr, David Hamburg, Rick Little, and Marian Wright Edelman remind us that considerable information is available, both in America and internationally, about how to design and deliver programs that will prevent the development of problem behaviors among youth and/or promote positive youth development.

However, the presence of this knowledge is not sufficient in and of itself to eliminate the problems facing our nation's youth. I believe that four additional points must be addressed.

First, and foremost, America must commit itself to developing a comprehensive and integrative youth development policy. As persuasively argued by Karen J. Pittman and Shepherd Zeldin (1994), this policy must be directed to the promotion of positive youth development, more so than even to prevention and, certainly, more so than to deterrence or remediation.

Second, then, and ideally within the context of this national youth development policy, resources must be available for sustaining programs shown, through appropriate evaluations, to be effective. Moreover, these resources must be used to increase the capacity of community members themselves to sustain these programs and to create community-wide, comprehensive, and integrative services that enhance the life chances of their children, adolescents, and families.

Third, communities must learn from each other. Although effective programs are ones that fit with the values and mores of a specific community, each time that a community wishes to institute a program promoting youth abstinence in sex or drug and alcohol use, a program enhancing engagement in safe sexual practices, a youth violence prevention program, or a program promoting school achievement, it need not start from scratch. Rather, we should seek to replicate or extend knowledge of effective programming in one community to other communities with similar interests or needs. Communities will benefit from knowledge about what are the *best practices* potentially available to them to address issues of concern about children and adolescents.

Fourth, then, we must bring university personnel into more effective collaborations with communities. Faculty associated with research and outreach or extension have the expertise to generate and disseminate knowledge about the best practices available; how replication may be achieved; how to evaluate—in a community-collaborative and program-formative manner—the youth programs in a given community; and how to ascertain, or "map," the assets and strengths present in a community, that is, the individual and institutional resources that may be useful in building and sustaining a specific program in a particular community.

I recognize, of course, that none of these four points will be easy to achieve. Indeed, as a member of a university faculty and, especially, given at this writing my almost two decades of experiences in land-grant universities, I am especially aware of the problems that must be addressed for universities to enter into long-term and truly collaborative partnerships with communities.

For instance, research and extension faculty do not typically collaborate with each other. Thus research and outreach have not ordinarily been integrated activities within American universities. In addition, community-collaborative research is not highly valued or rewarded in our nation's universities. Indeed, the ethos within many universities—even land-grant institutions—is to pursue academic agendas determined primarily by disciplinary concerns.

The problems of communities become salient, then, when they can be translated into the language of a discipline and when such translation can be coupled with, first, grant support for basic research or for a demonstration project and, typically, second, the potential for the publication of an article or a book. Unfortunately, however, when the funds in the grant are spent, when the demonstration project is over, or when sufficient information for the article or book is obtained, it is all too often the case that the university's and/or the faculty member's "interest" in the community problem also comes to an end.

This approach by universities and research faculty to participating in addressing the problems confronting our nation's children and adolescents has failed America. Indeed, the lack of a sustained and a genuine commitment to collaboratively addressing the problems of our nation's communities—*as the communities, and not the professoriate define them*—has led to a growing disaffection among the American public toward its universities. As Ernest L. Boyer (1990, 1994), of the Carnegie Foundation for the Advancement of Teaching, has noted, the American public increasingly sees universities and their professoriate to be elitist and societally disengaged. There is a growing question in the minds of many citizens about the wisdom of continuing to financially support institutions that have the potential to address community problems but, from the vantage point of the community, are not doing so.

When I take off my "hat" as professor and researcher and don my role as community member, as husband, and as father, I must admit that I too feel frustrated about the lack of adequate knowledge generation, knowledge transmission, and knowledge application aimed at addressing in a collaborative manner the needs of our communities, that is, aimed at outreach. I am concerned that the skills of researchers are not being more deeply integrated with the skills of university extension or other outreach colleagues for better knowledge generation and transmission to occur. And I too, quite frankly, feel that if universities are not going to be a greater part of the solution to the problems facing America's diverse youth, families, and communities, their access to public financial support should be sharply curtailed.

I choose to believe, however, that the current general character of universities' roles in addressing community-defined problems of children and adolescents is not a necessary or inevitable one. Indeed, as Boyer (1994) has noted, along with a tradition in America of university disinterest in community problems, there has also been a tradition—exemplified by the vision of land-grant institutions but, as well, present in non-land-grant state universities and colleges and, in some cases, private institutions—of a university devoted to addressing the practical problems of American life. Accordingly, if we can capitalize on the latter tradition, we may be able to create a means to bring universities into sustained collaborations with communities, with the diverse citizens, agencies, and institutions that will need to enter into coalitions if we are to adequately promote the positive development of our nation's youth.

One way to "capture the hearts" of American academics is to "capture their minds." I believe that if an intellectually sound, innovative, and useful model of scholarship can be presented to the professoriate—a model that promotes the integration of research and outreach, researchers and extension colleagues, and university and community—the probability of community-collaborative academic engagement with the problems besetting America's children and adolescents would be substantially enhanced.

The goal of this book, and indeed of much of my career over the past two decades, is to present such a model and, more important, to use the model as a means to understand both the problems of America's children and adolescents and the potential to promote positive youth development through policies and programs. Termed *developmental contextualism,* this model provides a theoretical frame for viewing the development of children and adolescents as occurring in relation to the specific features of their actual, *ecologically valid* context, that is, their specific family, neighborhoods, society, culture, physical environments, and even the particular point in history within which they live. Developmental contextualism sees human development as occurring, then, within a systematically changing and complex (that is, multilevel) system; as such, children and adolescents as much influence their contexts—for example, children as much affect their parents—as their contexts (their parents) influence them.

Developmental contextualism leads, then, to descriptions, of both the problems and the potential for healthy development of America's children and adolescents, that are associated with these bidirectional relationships between youth and their contexts. Moreover, to explain development, one must also turn to the system of relations between youth and their contexts. And, to test these explanations, one must change something about the actual context within which youth live. These changes constitute both experimental manipulations designed to test theoretical ideas about the variables that influence the course of human development *and* interventions aimed at changing for the better the life paths of children and adolescents.

Depending on the level of organization involved in these contextual ma-nipulations/interventions, we may label these planned changes into the course of human life as either policies or programs. Thus, when we evalu-ate the efficacy of these interventions in regard to the changes in the hu-man life course associated with them, we are learning something about the adequacy of particular policies and programs to effect desired changes among children and adolescents, and we are learning something very basic about how human development occurs through changing relations be-tween the developing person and his or her actual context. In other words, within developmental contextualism there is a synthesis of basic, theory-testing research and the applied scholarship associated with program and policy design, delivery, and evaluation.

Using developmental contextualism as a frame for both reviewing the dimensions of the contemporary crisis of America's children and adoles-cents and capitalizing on the potential for positive development present in the diverse youth, families, and communities of our nation, I propose an agenda for integrating research and outreach. Moreover, building on the seminal work of Dryfoos, Schorr, and Hamburg, I use developmental con-textualism to discuss both the features of successful prevention and devel-opment-enhancing programs for youth, and the principles that seem to be key in the design and implementation of such programs. Based again on the scholarship of Dryfoos, I illustrate the features and principles of suc-cessful youth programs by discussing the concept of *full-service schools*.

In addition, I discuss how the developmental contextual approach to integrating research and outreach can be used to assist universities in be-coming productive partners in community coalitions aimed at addressing the problems and potentials of children and adolescents. In this context, I focus on the changes in the cultures of both the academic campus and the community that will need to occur for effective and sustained university-community partnerships to be developed. However, I recognize that creation of the conditions affording such cultural changes will rest on the develop-ment of innovative academic and social policies, ones aimed, respectively, at providing incentives for universities to collaborate with communities and at establishing an integrative and comprehensive national youth policy.

In sum, then, my hope is that this book will increase awareness of both the problems besetting our nation's youth, families, and communities and, more important, I believe, the potentials that exist for positive youth de-velopment—potentials that may be actualized if there is an adoption of an integrative agenda of research, policy engagement, and program design, delivery, and evaluation. Moreover, it is my hope that this book will stimulate increases in the quantity and quality of collaborations among university research and extension colleagues and the diverse communities of our states and nation. I believe that such collaborations will be the essential feature of a new national agenda for our nation's children and adolescents, one pulling us all back from the precipice of generational destruction and enabling America to take a major step toward fulfilling the vision of the Children's Defense Fund, that is, to create a nation wherein "we will leave no child behind."

ACKNOWLEDGMENTS

There are always numerous people and institutions to thank in regard to the preparation of a book. In the case of this book, this debt seems to be especially true. First, I am grateful to my colleagues at National 4-H for asking me to prepare this book, providing constructive feedback throughout the process, and having the patience and good spirits to sit through several presentations of the ideas. Thus the support and assistance of Richard J. Sauer, President of National 4-H Council, Wendy Wheeler, Project Leader, National 4-H Council, and Nancy L. Valentine, National 4-H Program Leader, Extension Service, U.S. Department of Agriculture are gratefully acknowledged and deeply appreciated.

The generosity of several foundations and their commitment to America's youth, families, and communities also enabled this work to be initiated and completed. I am grateful to the support provided by the DeWitt Wallace-Reader's Digest Fund for its support of the National 4-H activities of which this book is a part; the W. K. Kellogg Foundation for supporting many of the activities of the Institute for Children, Youth, and Families at Michigan State University, activities that allowed several of the ideas presented in this book to be developed, refined, and implemented; and the Charles Stewart Mott Foundation and the Annie E. Casey Foundation for supporting major instances of the outreach scholarship that is occurring at the Institute for Children, Youth, and Families, that is, the sort of scholarship called for within this book.

If my work at the Institute for Children, Youth, and Families has enabled me to develop the ideas I present in this book—and indeed it has—

this stimulation has occurred because of the superb colleagues and excellent students I have been fortunate to have, both at the institute and across the Michigan State University campus. Thus I am grateful to L. Annette Abrams, Mary L. Andrews, Jes Asmussen, Carla L. Barnes, Jenny T. Bond, Jeanne A. Brickman, Timothy S. Bynum, Domini Castellino, Alina R. Chacon, Linda K. Chapel, Robert L. Church, Kenneth E. Corey, George Cornell, Stephen C. Curtin, Hiram Davis, Marylee Davis, James Dearing, W. Patrick Dickson, Clayton C. Dowling, James Dye, Hiram E. Fitzgerald, Melissa A. Freel, Robert J. Griffore, Oran Hesterman, Leah Cox Hoopfer, Rick C. Hula, Daniel Ilgen, Steven Kaagan, David J. Kallen, Joanne G. Keith, Karen Klomparens, Jack H. Knott, Marjorie J. Kostelnik, Harriette P. McAdoo, John L. McAdoo, Marvin H. McKinney, John Metzler, Julia R. Miller, John B. Molidor, Charles W. Ostrom, Julie F. Parks, Daniel F. Perkins, Penelope Peterson, Celeste Sturdevant Reed, Lee Anne W. Roman, Lorilee Sandmann, Lawrence B. Schiamberg, Vernal Seefeldt, Harvey Sparks, Linda Spence, Linda Stanford, Christine Stephens, Carl S. Taylor, Patterson A. Terry, Charles Thompson, James Tiedje, Linda Beth Tiedje, Francisco A. Villarruel, James C. Votruba, William B. Weil, and Bruce E. Wilson for all their stimulation, support, and collaboration. I want to especially thank the colleagues who provided me with their comments about this book: Domini Castellino, Robert L. Church, Hiram E. Fitzgerald, Joanne G. Keith, Jacqueline V. Lerner, Julia R. Miller, Charles W. Ostrom, Daniel F. Perkins, Nancy L. Valentine, Francisco A. Villarruel, and Wendy Wheeler.

I believe that it is because Michigan State has made a university-wide commitment to integrating research and outreach for children, adolescents, and families and has created a campus climate that promotes both consideration and implementation of the integrative ideas presented in this book that the institute has been able to initiate and make progress in the agenda for community-collaborative research and outreach discussed in this book. Here the vision, values, energy, creativity, and leadership of James C. Votruba, Vice Provost for University Outreach; Julia R. Miller, Dean of the College of Human Ecology and Chair of the institute's Executive Board of Deans; Gail L. Imig, Director, MSU Extension; Robert L. Church, Assistant Vice Provost for University Outreach; Leah Cox Hoopfer, Program Director, Children, Youth, and Family Programs; and Frank A. Fear, Chair of the Provost's Committee on University Outreach have been vital to the progress of the institute and, as well, to the creation at

Michigan State of a model of university-community collaboration aimed at promoting the healthy development of children and adolescents.

Moreover, the commitment to outreach scholarship and its vision for children, adolescents, and families that exist among the members of the institute's Executive Board of Deans have made essential contributions to the development of the agenda of the institute. Thus I am grateful for the wisdom and collegiality of William S. Abbett, Dean, College of Human Medicine; Erwin P. Bettinghaus, Dean, College of Communication Arts and Sciences; Marilyn Rothert, Dean, College of Nursing; Kenneth E. Corey, Dean, College of Social Science; Joe T. Darden, Dean, Urban Affairs Programs; Carole Ames, Dean, College of Education; Percy A. Pierre, Vice President for Research; Fred L. Poston, Dean, College of Agriculture and Natural Resources; Douglas L. Wood, Dean, College of Osteopathic Medicine; Julia R. Miller, Dean, College of Human Ecology; James C. Votruba, Vice Provost for University Outreach; Gail L. Imig, Director, MSU Extension; and Arnold Revzin, Assistant Vice President for Research.

I have also been fortunate to have had the opportunity to learn a great deal from the community collaborators with whom I have had the privilege to work during my time at Michigan State. I am grateful to all of these fine people. They have taught me not only what a university might contribute to the lives of children, adolescents, families, and the communities it serves but also how much a university can learn from the communities with which it collaborates. In particular, I would like to extend my special thanks to Camille Abood, Attorney, Abood, Abood, & Rheamue; Velma Allen, Director, Community Affairs, Mott Children's Health Center; James F. Anderton, Jr., Chairman and CEO, Summit Holdings Corporation; Vernice Davis Anthony, Director, Michigan Department of Public Health; Pam Barckholtz, Saginaw Community Mental Health; Antonio Benavides, Executive Director, Cristo Rey Community Center; Robert G. Berning, President, Capital Area United Way; Connie Binsfeld, Lt. Governor, State of Michigan; Barbara Bowman, Vice President for Academic Programs, Erikson Institute; Jeanne A. Brickman, Children, Youth, and Family Programs, Michigan State University; Norman A. Brown, President, W. K. Kellogg Foundation; Andrea Colliar, Department of Public Health; Dolores Cook, MSU Board of Trustees; Elizabeth Dilley, Executive Director, Grand Rapids Education Foundation; Chris Fedewa, Lansing Mayor's Committee on Children, Youth, and Families; Joel Ferguson, Chair, MSU Board of Trustees;

Cele Gerber, Director, Michigan Capitol Girl Scouts Council; Dorothy Gonzales, MSU Board of Trustees; William G. Gonzales, President and CEO, Butterworth Hospital; Michael G. Harrison, Circuit Court Judge, Ingham County Circuit Court; James K. Haveman, Director, Michigan Department of Mental Health; Randall Hekman, Executive Director, Michigan Family Forum; David Hollister, Mayor, City of Lansing; Chris Holman, Publisher, *Greater Lansing Business Monthly*; Robert Ivory, President, Michigan United Way; Gene Keilitz, United Way of Michigan; Kathleen L. Kissman, Assistant Director, Michigan State University Alumni Association; Judith Lindsay, Codirector, Perinatal Outreach Program, Butterworth Hospital; Rick R. Little, Secretary General, International Youth Foundation; Hanmin Liu, President, United States–China Educational Institute; Cyndi Mark, Children, Youth, and Family Program, Michigan State University; Aretha Marshall, Executive Director, Middle Level Education, Detroit Schools; Donna Massie, Department Head, Developmental Assessment and Collaborative Care, Mott Children's Health Center; Russell G. Mawby, Chairman and CEO, W. K. Kellogg Foundation; Jack K. Mawdsley, Program Director, W. K. Kellogg Foundation; Paul McConaughy, Vice President, Research and Communications, Capital Area United Way; Jean McDonald, Chair, Ingham County Board of Commissioners; Larry Meyer, Vice Chairman and CEO, Michigan Retailers Association; Gerald H. Miller, Director, Michigan Department of Social Services; Joseph S. Moore, Codirector, Perinatal Outreach Program, Butterworth Hospital; Michael Murphy, Pastor, St. Stephens Community Church; Carol M. O'Laughlin, Program Director, International Youth Foundation; Donald Owens, Judge of Probate, Ingham County Probate Court; Beverly Pacynski, Bay–Arenac Intermediate School District; Douglas M. Paterson, Chief, Division of Child and Adolescent Health; Roy E. Peterson, President, Mott Children's Health Center; Lana Pollack, State Senator, 18th District; John Pollard, Executive Director, Black Child and Family Institute, Lansing; William L. Randall, Chairman Emeritus, First Bank–Milwaukee; James Ray, Assistant Superintendent, Flint Community Schools; Dorothy Reynolds, President, Flint Community Foundation; Nanette Reynolds, Director, State of Michigan, Department of Civil Rights; Ethel Rios de Betancourt, President, Puerto Rico Community Foundation; Osvaldo Rivera, Acting Dean, Student Affairs, Macomb Community College; Kent Roberts, Youth and Family Coordinator, Sturgis Community Youth and Family Agency; Barbara Roberts Mason, Founder and President of the Black

Child and Family Institute and Member, Michigan Board of Education; Theresa C. Robinson, Project Coordinator, Beecher 102 Teen Health Center, Beecher, Michigan; Thomas Rutledge, Department Head, Behavior, Mott Children's Health Center; Barbara J. Sawyer-Koch, MSU Board of Trustees; Shelly Schadewald, Project Coordinator, Michigan Abstinence Partnership; Karen Schrock, Chief, Center for Substance Abuse Services; Donald Shebuski, Ingham Intermediate School District; Paul Sheehan, Executive Director, Michigan Council for Maternal and Child Health; John D. Shingleton, MSU Board of Trustees; Leonard W. Smith, President, Skillman Foundation; Debbie Stabenow, State Senator, 24th District, State of Michigan; J. Mark Sullivan, Executive Director, Michigan 4-C Association; Betty Tableman, Director, Prevention Services; Bob Traxler, MSU Board of Trustees; Willard Walker, Lansing Associate of Black Organizations; Robert E. Weiss, MSU Board of Trustees; Judson Werbelow, Attorney, Dickenson, Wright, Moon, VanDusen & Freeman; H. Stephen Williams, Vice President, Clinical Affairs, Mott Children's Health Center; Winston Williams, National African American Youth Leadership Council; James Wotring, Michigan Interagency Family Preservation Coordinator; and Terri D. Wright, Chief, Bureau of Child and Family Services.

There is another group of academic and community colleagues to whom I owe a special debt: the members of the institute's Visiting Committee. These colleagues—Kathryn E. Barnard, Professor and Associate Dean for Academic Program, University of Washington; Jeanne Brooks-Gunn, Director, Teachers College, Columbia University; Erik P. Butler, President, Bay State Skills; David L. Featherman, President, Social Science Research Council; Michael Huberman, Visiting Professor, Harvard Graduate Education and Senior Research Associate, New England Laboratory for School Improvement; Michael E. Lamb, Chief, Section of Social and Emotional Development, NICHD; David Magnusson, Chair, Psykologiska Institutionen; Edward L. Palmer, President, World Media Partners; Karen J. Pittman, Vice President and Director, Center for Youth Development and Policy Research; Richard J. Sauer, President, National 4-H Council; Ranier K. Silbereisen, Professor at the University of Jena, Germany; Graham B. Spanier, Chancellor, University of Nebraska–Lincoln and Chair of the ICYF Visiting Committee; and Bennie Stovall, past Executive Director of Detroit Children's Aid Society—lend their expertise and wisdom to enhancing the institute's programs of outreach scholarship. I am very grateful for all their efforts on behalf of the institute.

Finally, neither the institute nor the university nor the communities of our state, nation, and world could succeed in their attempts to promote a new vision of outreach scholarship unless the leadership of Michigan State University was deeply committed to this goal. Michigan State is fortunate to have as its President, M. Peter McPherson, and as its Provost and Vice President for Academic Affairs, Lou Anna Kimsey Simon. These leaders have both the vision and administrative skills to forge for Michigan State a new path: the creation of a community-collaborative, outreach university. I am grateful to have the opportunity to work with them in this endeavor, and I am deeply appreciative of the personal and administrative support they have given to the institute and to me.

As will be evident to the readers of this book, numerous scholars from outside of Michigan State University contributed immensely to the ideas I present. I am grateful to all of them for the important and stimulating work they have produced. In particular, I want to acknowledge my great debt to Joy G. Dryfoos, Lisbeth B. Schorr, David A. Hamburg, Rick Little, the Center for the Study of Social Policy, and the Children's Defense Fund and its President, Marian Wright Edelman. Their scholarship is central to the information presented in this book, and their advocacy for children and adolescents represents a call to conscience for all of America.

I also want to thank the several other colleagues who, over the years, have helped me elaborate and refine the ideas associated with the developmental contextual and university-community collaborative perspectives that frame this book. Thus I am grateful to Paul B. Baltes, Richard Birkel, Marc Bornstein, Ernest L. Boyer, Orville G. Brim, Jr., Urie Bronfenbrenner, Geraldine Brookins, Jeanne Brooks-Gunn, Nancy A. Busch-Rossnagel, Stella Chess, Anne Colby, William Damon, John DiBiaggio, Roger A. Dixon, Patricia L. East, Glen H. Elder, Jr., Doris Entwistle, David L. Featherman, Celia B. Fisher, Donald H. Ford, Nancy Galambos, Gilbert J. Gottlieb, Gary Greenberg, John W. Hagen, Beatrix A. Hamburg, Stuart T. Hauser, Donald J. Hernandez, E. Mavis Hetherington, Donald F. Hultsch, Francine H. Jacobs, Jasna Jovanovic, Jerome Kagen, Bernard Kaplan, Claire B. Kopp, Sam J. Korn, Kurt Kreppner, Deanna Kuhn, Michael E. Lamb, Kathleen Lenerz, Jacqueline V. Lerner, Michael Lewis, John L. McKnight, Vonnie McLoyd, Paul H. Mussen, Willis F. Overton, Marion Perlmutter, Karen J. Pittman, Hayne W. Reese, Arnold J. Sameroff, K. Warner Schaie, T. C. Schneirla, John E. Schulenberg, David K. Scott, Diane Scott-Jones, Lonnie R. Sherrod, Graham B. Spanier, Margaret Beale

Spencer, Ruby Takanishi, Ethel Tobach, Alexander Thomas, Jonathan Tubman, Fred Vondracek, Seymour Wapner, Valora Washington, Michael Windle, Sheldon H. White, Sherry Willis, and Robert A. Zucker. In addition, I want to especially express my sincere gratitude to Joy G. Dryfoos, Richard J. Sauer, and Justin S. Lerner for their graciousness in writing forewords to this book.

Finally, but most important, I am grateful for my own children, adolescents, and family. The love and support I receive from my wife, Jacqueline, and from Justin, Blair, and Jarrett provide my energy, motivation, and hope. It is to them that this book, and all my efforts on behalf of youth and families everywhere, are dedicated.

NOTE

1. This quote and quotes in following chapters from *Today's Children: Creating a Future for a Generation in Crisis,* by D. A. Hamburg, 1992, New York: Times Books, copyright © 1992 by Dr. David Hamburg are reprinted with permission of Times Books, a division of Random House, Inc.

1

The Contemporary Crises of America's Children and Adolescents

Across the communities of our nation, children are dying—from violence, from drug and alcohol use and abuse, from unsafe sex, from poor nutrition, and from the sequelae of persistent and pervasive poverty (Dryfoos, 1990; Hamburg, 1992; Huston, 1992; Lerner, 1993a, 1993b; McKinney, Abrams, Terry, & Lerner, 1994; Schorr, 1988; Wilson, 1987). And if our children are not dying, their life chances are being squandered—by school failure, underachievement, and dropout; by crime; by teenage pregnancy and parenting; by lack of job preparedness; by prolonged welfare dependency; by challenges to their health (e.g., lack of immunizations, inadequate screening for disabilities, insufficient prenatal care, and lack of sufficient infant and childhood medical services); and by the feelings of despair and hopelessness that pervade the lives of children whose parents have lived in poverty and who see themselves as having little opportunity to do better, that is, to have a life marked by societal respect, achievement, and opportunity (Dryfoos, 1990; Huston, 1992; Huston, McLoyd, & Coll, 1994).

There are numerous manifestations of the severity and breadth of the problems besetting our nation's youth, families, and communities. To illustrate, consider the four major categories of risk behaviors in late childhood and adolescence (Dryfoos, 1990):

1

- Drug and alcohol use and abuse
- Unsafe sex, teenage pregnancy, and teenage parenting
- School failure, underachievement, and dropout
- Delinquency, crime, and violence

Clearly, participation in any one of these behaviors would diminish a youth's life chances. Indeed, engagement in some of these behaviors would eliminate the young person's chances of even having a life. Such risks to the life chances of America's children and adolescents are occurring, unfortunately, at historically unprecedented levels.

Today, in America, there are approximately 28 million children and adolescents between the ages of 10 and 17 years. About 50% of these youth engage in *two or more* of the above-noted categories of risk behaviors (Dryfoos, 1990). Moreover, 10% of our nation's youth engage in *all* of the four categories of risk behaviors (Dryfoos, 1990).

Thus these data indicate that risk behaviors are highly interrelated in children and adolescents. Half of our nation's youth are at least at moderate risk as a consequence of engaging in two or more risk behaviors. And one American youth in every 10 is at very high risk as a consequence of "doing it all," of engaging in behaviors associated with every category of risk behavior.

ILLUSTRATIONS OF RISK BEHAVIORS

Within each of the categories of risk behavior, there are a burgeoning number of indications of the extensiveness of the problems confronting our nation's youth. Information derived from several recent publications—for instance, by the Center for the Study of Social Policy (e.g., the *Kids Count Data Book* from 1992 and 1993); the Children's Defense Fund (Simons, Finlay, & Yang, 1991); the Carnegie Council on Adolescent Development (1989) and the Carnegie Corporation of New York (1992, 1994); and scholars such as Dryfoos (1990), Hamburg (1992), Mincy (1994), Hernandez (1993), and a committee of the National Research Council (1993)—provides several dramatic illustrations of the breadth and depth of these problems.

Considering the category of drug and alcohol use and abuse, the following has been reported:

- In 1990, about 25% of 12- to 17-year-olds and more than 50% of 18- to 25-year-olds had used illicit drugs.
- About 10% of sixth graders have initiated alcohol use. In addition, about 25% of 12- to 14-year-olds and more than 50% of America's seventh graders are currently users. About 40% drink weekly.
- About 92% of high school seniors report some experience with alcohol, and one third use alcohol daily. In addition, one third are *binge drinkers,* which is defined as having five or more drinks in a row.
- About 66% of high school seniors have some experience with cigarettes, and 19% smoke cigarettes daily.

Moreover, in regard to behaviors involved in the risk category of unsafe sex, teenage pregnancy, and teenage parenting, current information indicates:

- Across the adolescent years, 80% of males and 70% of females initiate sexual intercourse; 20% of these youth have four or more sexual partners.
- Youth between 15 and 19 years account for 25% of the sexually transmitted disease (STD) cases each year. Moreover, 6.4% of adolescent runaways (of which, as will be noted below, there are between 750,000 and 1,000,000 each year in America) have positive serum tests for the AIDS virus. These runaway youth often engage in unsafe sex, prostitution, and intravenous drug use. Thus each year in America up to 64,000 time bombs are going out onto the streets of our towns and cities and spreading a disease that will kill them and the other people with whom they engage in unsafe sexual and drug-use-related behaviors.
- One million adolescents each year become pregnant; about half have babies. Indeed, about every minute, an American adolescent has a baby.
- Of adolescents who give birth, 46% go on welfare within four years; of *unmarried* adolescents who give birth, 73% go on welfare within four years.
- By age 18, 25% of American females have been pregnant at least once.
- About 40,000 babies are born each year to unwed mothers less than 15 years of age.
- In 1991, 531,591 babies were born to adolescents.
- Of the adolescents who became mothers in 1991, 69% were unmarried.
- African American unwed females, aged 15 to 19 years, have a birth rate of about 118 per 1,000; the corresponding rates for White non-Latino and Latino unwed females in this age range are about 43 per 1,000 and about 107 per 1,000, respectively.
- By age 19, 15% of African American males have fathered a child; the corresponding rates for White non-Latinos and for Latinos are about 7% and 11%, respectively. Moreover, most of these men are absentee fathers; this typically results in their babies being born into and living in single-parent,

female-head-of-household families. As will be explained below, there is a very high probability that such households will be poor ones, and thus the children in such settings are likely to experience the several negative effects of living in poverty.

In turn, in regard to the category of school failure, underachievement, and dropout, current information indicates:

- About 25% of the approximately 40 million children and adolescents enrolled in America's 82,000 public elementary and secondary schools are at risk for school failure.
- Each year about 700,000 youth drop out of school. About 25% of all 18- and 19-year-olds have not graduated from high school.
- At any point in time, about 18% of all 18- to 24-year-old dropouts and 30% of 23- to 25-year-old dropouts are under supervision of the criminal justice system. Among African Americans, the corresponding percentages are about 50% and 75%, respectively.
- During the 1980s, school drop-out rates for African Americans living in inner cities increased to between 40% and 50%.
- High school drop-out rates are 300% higher among poor young adults, of all race or ethnic backgrounds, than they are among nonpoor young adults.
- African Americans and Native Americans are about 200% more likely than are European Americans to be high school dropouts. Latinos are about 300% more likely.
- African American youth graduate from high school at about the same rate as do European American youth. Across the nation, the percentage of European American and African American males aged 18 to 24 years who have not completed high school is about 24% and 32%, respectively. However, the number of years needed to graduate from high school is greater among African Americans.
- About 4.5 million 10- to 14-year-olds are one or more years behind in their modal grade level.
- African American and Latino teenagers are more likely than are European Americans to be two or more grades behind in school.
- In 1986, 57% of 10- to 15-year-old African Americans were two or more years behind their grade level.
- In 1989, 75% of African American 25- to 34-year-olds who completed high school worked, whereas 90% of European American high school graduates in this age range worked. African Americans who worked full time and full year earned 81% as much as their European American counterparts.

- A male high school dropout earns $260,000 less than a high school graduate and contributes $78,000 less in taxes over his lifetime. For a female dropout, the comparable figures are $200,000 and $60,000.
- Unemployment rates for dropouts are more than double those of high school graduates.
- Each added year of secondary education reduces the probability of public welfare dependency in adulthood by 35%.

Finally, in regard to the risk category of delinquency, crime, and violence, information currently available indicates:

- Youth, aged 13 to 21 years, accounted for 35.5% of all non-traffic-related arrests in the United States during the 1980s, although this age group was only 14.3% of the population.
- As noted above, between 750,000 and 1,000,000 youth run away from home each year.
- In the mid-1980s, 1.7 million arrests occurred among 10- to 17-year-olds. More than 500,000 of those arrested were 14 years of age or younger, and 46,000 were under age 10.
- In 1991, 130,000 arrests of youth aged 10 to 17 years were made for rape, robbery, homicide, or aggravated assault. This figure represents an increase of 48% since 1986.
- At any point in time, about 20% of all African American youth are involved with the criminal justice system.
- Between 1980 and 1990, arrest rates of African American adolescents charged with weapons violations, murder, and aggravated assault increased by 102%, 145%, and 89%, respectively.
- African Americans experience rates of rape, aggravated assault, and armed robbery that are approximately 25% higher than those for European Americans; rates of motor vehicle theft are about 70% higher; and rates of robbery victimization are about 150% higher. Finally, rates of African American homicide are typically between 600% to 700% higher.
- African American males are at particular risk for being victims of violent crime. For example, in 1988, the firearm death rates among 15- to 19-year-old and among 20- to 24-year-old African American males were about 80 per 100,000 and about 125 per 100,000, respectively; the corresponding rates for European American 15- to 19-year-old and 20- to 24-year-old males were about 30 per 100,000 for both age groups, respectively. In turn, in 1988, homicide death rates among African American 15- to 19-year-old and 20- to 24-year-old males were about 80 per 100,000 and about 120 per 100,000,

respectively; the corresponding rates for European American males in the two age ranges were about 5 per 100,000 and about 18 per 100,000, respectively.

TEMPORAL TRENDS IN RISK BEHAVIORS

The above-noted data regarding the prevalence of risk behaviors indicate that the current status of American youth is exceedingly problematic. Indeed, these data suggest that nothing short of a "generational time bomb" (Lerner, 1993a) is confronting American society. With so many of our nation's youth beset with so many instances of behavioral risk, America is on the verge of shortly losing much of its next generation, that is, the human capital on which the future of our nation relies (Hamburg, 1992; Lerner, 1993a, 1993b). Moreover, the "fuse" on the time bomb appears to be growing appreciably shorter: Several sources of data indicate that many of the key problems of American youth are increasing at relatively rapid rates.

For instance, information from the 1993 *Kids Count Data Book,* published by the Center for the Study of Social Policy, indicates that, between 1985 and 1992, many of the above-noted problems of children and adolescents grew substantially worse. For instance, the rate of violent deaths for 15- to 19-year-olds increased by 13%, whereas for European American youth this increased rate was 10% and for African American 15- to 19-year-olds it was 78%. In addition, the percentage of youth graduating from high school decreased by 4%, the percentage of all births that were to single teenagers increased by 16% (and involved a 26% increase among European American youth and no increase among African American teenagers), the arrest rate among 10- to 17-year-olds increased by 48% (with European Americans increasing by 58% and African Americans by 29%), and the number of children in single-parent families increased by 9% (with the corresponding rates for European American and for African American children increasing by 9% and by 6%, respectively).

As noted above, these latter family structure changes are associated with both poverty and the interrelation of risk behaviors among children and adolescents. As noted by Schorr (1988), child poverty is the single most damaging structural feature of American society affecting the quality of youth development. Accordingly, it is important to discuss the prevalence and temporal trends associated with poverty among American youth.

CHILD AND YOUTH POVERTY

Child and youth poverty exacerbates the risk behaviors of adolescents, and poverty is a growing problem for America's youth (Huston, 1992; Lerner, 1993a). By the end of the 1980s, approximately 20% of America's children and adolescents were poor (Huston, 1992; Huston et al., 1994; Simons et al., 1991). Moreover, data in the *Kids Count Data Book* (Center for the Study of Social Policy, 1992) indicate that, during the 1980s, the percentage of children living in poverty in the United States increased by 22%. Indeed, this national trend was present in 40 states and continues to increase across the nation (Huston, 1992). Furthermore, of the 12 million American children under the age of 3, 25% live in poor families (Carnegie Corporation of New York, 1994). In addition, whereas the number of children under age 6 decreased by 10% between 1971 and 1991, the number of poor children in this age group *increased by 60%* (Carnegie Corporation of New York, 1994).

Child poverty occurs in all geographic regions of America. In fact, the rates of poverty in rural areas of the Unites States are as high as those in the inner cities (Huston, 1992; Jensen, 1988). Moreover, poor families in rural areas receive fewer welfare benefits and are less likely to live in states that provide Aid to Families With Dependent Children (AFDC) (Huston, 1992; Jensen, 1988).

However, it must be stressed that the probability of being a poor child is not equal across racial or ethnic groups. According to the *Kids Count Data Book* (Center for the Study of Social Policy, 1993), during the 1987-1991 period, the average percentage of European American, African American, and Latino children who were poor was 11.4%, 44.1%, and 37.9%, respectively. Moreover, among Latino groups, Puerto Rican children experienced the highest rate of poverty (40.4%) and Cuban children experienced the lowest rate (19.7%) (U.S. Bureau of the Census, 1991). In addition, it should be noted that, as reported in 1991 by the U.S. Bureau of the Census, Asian children and Native American children experienced rates of poverty of 16.7% and 24.9%, respectively.

The percentages of children in poverty during the 1987-1991 period represent increases in the rates of poverty over the past 10 years for all racial/ethnic groups. For example, from 1979 to 1989, child poverty grew worse by 9% for European Americans, by 5% for African Americans, and by 25% for Latinos, respectively (Center for the Study of Social Policy,

1993). In terms of absolute numbers, data from the 1990 Census indicate that 5.9 million European American children lived in poverty, whereas the corresponding numbers of African Americans, Asian Americans, Native Americans, and Latinos were 3.7 million, 346,000, 260,000, and 2.4 million, respectively (Children's Defense Fund, 1992).

In short, as noted by Huston (1992), race is the most striking and disturbing distinction between children whose poverty is chronic and children for whom poverty is transitory. For instance, Duncan (1992) reports data from the Panel Study on Income Dynamics indicating that the average African American child in the study spent 5.5 years in poverty; in turn, the average non-African American child in the study spent only 0.9 of a year in poverty. Furthermore, as with race and ethnicity, poverty is not equally distributed across age groups. In 1989, about 20% of children younger than age 6 were poor, and the corresponding rate of poverty for 6- to 17-year-olds was about 17%. In turn, the rates for Americans aged 18 to 64 years or aged 65 years or older were about 11% and 13%, respectively (Children's Defense Fund, 1992).

The sequelae of poverty for children and adolescents are devastating. Indeed, as Hamburg (1992) notes: "Almost every form of childhood damage is far more prevalent among the poor—from increased infant mortality, gross malnutrition, recurrent and untreated health problems, and child abuse in the early years, to education disability, low achievement, delinquency, early pregnancy, alcohol and drug abuse, and failure to become economically self-sufficient" (p. 48). Similarly, as Schorr (1988) stresses, poverty creates several "rotten outcomes" of youth development. For example, poverty is associated with early school failure, unemployability, long-term welfare dependency, violent crime, and feelings of hopelessness and despair (McLoyd & Wilson, 1992; Schorr, 1988, 1992). Furthermore, McLoyd and Wilson (1992) and Klerman (1992) find that poor children live at high risk for low self-confidence, conduct problems, depression, and peer conflict. In addition, poor children are at risk for encountering severe health problems, for example, infant mortality; lack of immunization against common childhood diseases; and physical abuse, neglect, and unintended injury (Carnegie Corporation of New York, 1994; McLoyd & Wilson, 1992).

Moreover, as compared to their nonpoor age-mates, poor youth are 50% more likely to have physical or mental disability, almost twice as likely to have not visited a doctor or dentist in the most recent two years of their lives, 300% more likely to be high school dropouts, and significantly more likely to be victims of violence (Simons et al., 1991). In addition, several familial risk factors are associated with both child poverty and a key covariate of poverty—poor school achievement.

To illustrate, three maternal risk factors are associated with a child's living in poverty and, as well, with a child's being in the lower half of his or her school class. These risk factors are that the mother (a) has fewer than 12 years of schooling, (b) is not married to the child's father, and (c) was less than 20 years old when she had her first child. That these risk factors are of moment for family life and for child development can be illustrated by reference to other *Kids Count Data Book* (Center for the Study of Social Policy, 1993) information linking these three risk factors to child poverty and to school achievement. Among all 7- to 12-year-old children living in America, there was a probability of .79 that the child would be poor if all three risk factors were present. Similarly, the probability of being in the lower half of one's school class was .58 if all these three factors were present. In turn, when any two of these risk factors were present the probability of being poor or of being in the bottom half of one's school class was .48 and .53, respectively. The corresponding probabilities involving the presence of only one risk factor were .26 and .47, respectively. Finally, when none of these risk factors were present the probability of 7- to 12-year-old children being poor or being in the lower half of their class was .08 and .30, respectively.

Across the 1980s, the probability increased that there would be a link between child poverty and the presence of maternal risk factors. That is, as the poverty rates of America's children worsen, exceeding now all other major industrialized nations (Huston, 1992), the structure of the family is also changing in ways that have placed poor children and parents at greater risk for problems of family life and individual development. For instance, during the 1980s there was a 13% increase in the number of children living in single-parent families, a trend present in 44 states. Thus, during the 1987-1991 period, 18.1%, 30%, and 56.7% of European American, Latino, and African American children, respectively, lived in single-parent households (Center for the Study of Social Policy, 1992). Overall, approximately 25% of America's youth live in single-parent (and, typically, female-headed) families, and poverty rates among female-headed, single-parent or male-headed, single-parent families are much higher (46.8% and 23.2%, respectively) than among two-parent families (9.0%) (Center for the Study of Social Policy, 1993; Hernandez, 1993). Indeed, the poverty rates in single-parent households were, by the beginning of the 1990s, 29.8% for European American families, 50.6% for African American families, and 53% for Latino families (U.S. Department of Commerce, 1991). Because the income of female-headed, single-parent households is often three or more times lower than two-parent households and is also lower than single-parent, male-headed households, the fact that increasing numbers of children live in these family structures means that the financial resources to support parenting are less likely to be available (Center for the Study of Social Policy, 1993).

Moreover, in 1990, 90.3% of children were living with their parents, 7.3% were living with other relatives, and 2.3% were living outside of the family (Center for the Study of Social Policy, 1992). However, only 41.9% of African American children, 67.7% of Latino children, and 78.5% of European American children between the ages of 10 and 14 lived with both their parents (Simons et al., 1991). In turn, between the ages of 15 and 17, only 41%, 63%, and 76% of African American, Latino, and European American children, respectively, lived in two-parent households (Simons et al., 1991).

As a means to summarize the costs—not only to youth but to all of America as well—of pervasive child and adolescent poverty, we may note Hamburg's (1992) view that

> not only are many more children growing up in poverty than was the case a decade or two ago, but many more are mired in persistent, intractable poverty with no realistic hope of escape. They are profoundly lacking in constructively oriented social-support networks to promote their education and health. They have very few models of competence. They are bereft of visible economic opportunity. The fate of these young people is not merely a tragedy for them, but for the entire nation: A growing fraction of our potential work force consists of seriously disadvantaged people who will have little if any prospect of acquiring the necessary competence to revitalize the economy. If we cannot bring ourselves to feel compassion for these young people on a personal level, we must at least recognize that our economy and our society will suffer along with them. Their loss is our loss. (p. 10)

ADDRESSING THE CRISIS THROUGH
AN INTEGRATIVE THEORY OF HUMAN DEVELOPMENT

Given the number of children that today are at such profound levels of risk, we are faced as a society with a crisis so broad that the entire fabric of American society is in serious jeopardy (Simons et al., 1991). With so many of our nation's communities facing the likelihood of losing much of their next generation to one or more of the several high-risk behaviors increasingly present among our nation's youth, all of our children, whether they themselves engage in given risk behaviors, nevertheless, in effect, live in risk—of experiencing the adverse economic and employment conditions associated with living in a nation that is increasingly globally uncompetitive, has a diminished pool of future leaders, offers lowered standards of living, requires lower expectations about life chances, and, in fact, provides fewer and fewer opportunities for healthy and wholesome development (Lerner, 1993a).

Simply, America is wasting its most precious resource: the human capital represented by its children (Hamburg, 1992; Lerner, 1993a, 1993b; Lerner & Miller, 1993). And this destruction of human capital is a problem that cuts across race, ethnicity, gender, and rural or urban environments (Center for the Study of Social Policy, 1992, 1993; Simons et al., 1991). Accordingly, all of us, all Americans, and certainly all of our children and adolescents, are now and for the foreseeable future confronted by this crisis of youth development. Of course, the pervasiveness of this crisis does not diminish the need to prioritize our efforts. In fact, as will be discussed in Chapter 5, results of evaluation studies of preventive interventions indicate that great success can occur with programs directed to youth and families most in need (Dryfoos, 1990, 1994, in press; Hamburg, 1992; Schorr, 1988). Nevertheless, the breadth of the problems affecting our nation's youth requires that we see the issues we face as pertaining to all of us and not to only a segment or a subgroup of America.

Yet, despite the magnitude of this crisis confronting all the children of our nation, it is still the case that the preponderant majority of child development research is not focused on the behavioral risks confronting the diverse children of America; as a consequence, there are also relatively few developmental studies of child poverty and its sequelae. In fact, as will be discussed in Chapter 3, most studies published in the leading scientific journals in child development focus on investigations of European American, middle-class children (Fisher & Brennan, 1992; Graham, 1992; Hagen, Paul, Gibb, & Wolters, 1990). Moreover, most of these studies appraise children in laboratory settings, as compared to real-life ones, and do not address topics that are relevant to developing, delivering, or sustaining programs preventing either risk behaviors and/or the sequelae of persistent and pervasive poverty (Fisher & Brennan, 1992; Graham, 1992; McKinney et al., 1994; McLoyd, 1994).

As such, there is a considerable substantive distance between the work of many of America's child developmentalists and the problems facing the children of America (Graham, 1992; McLoyd, 1994). A similar gap exists between, on the one hand, those who seek to develop policies and programs that will help children lead better lives within their families and communities and, on the other, the scientists who can provide the intellectual base on which to build these endeavors.

These gaps, between the major foci of contemporary child development research and the needs of poor American children, families, and communities (Graham, 1992; McLoyd, 1994), exist despite the presence of alternative models for science and for outreach. In a report by the Michigan State University Provost's Committee on University Outreach (1993), outreach was conceived of as a form of scholarship that involves "the generation, transmission, application, and preservation of knowledge for the direct benefit of audiences to whom and for whom the university seeks to extend itself in ways that are consistent with university and unit missions" (p. 2). In other words, outreach involves the generation, transmission, application, or preservation of scholarship for purposes developed collaboratively with communities served by the university (Lerner & Miller, 1993; Lerner et al., 1994). When outreach scholarship is conducted in regard to children, their families, and/or their communities—or, more generally, in regard to human development—it may be defined as the "systematic synthesis of research and application to describe, explain, and promote optimal developmental outcomes in individuals and families as they develop along the life cycle" (Fisher & Lerner, 1994, p. 4). As shall be discussed in Chapter 3, this instance of outreach scholarship has been termed by Fisher and Lerner (1994) as *applied developmental science.*

Here, however, it is important to note that this view of outreach scholarship in the field of human development emerged within land-grant institutions' colleges of home economics, human ecology, family and consumer sciences, and human development (Lerner & Miller, 1993; Miller & Lerner, 1994). The perspectives about human development produced in these institutions have provided a vision of scholarship that integrates research and outreach (Boyer, 1990, 1994; Enarson, 1989; Lynton & Elman, 1987), a vision consistent with a 1991 statement of the National Council of Administrators of Home Economics Programs stressing that

> the mission of the profession in higher education is to conduct research and provide education programs that are integrative and are focused on reciprocal relationships among individuals, families, and their near environments toward improvement of the human condition within a dynamic world community. (p. 5)

A theory of child and family development—*developmental contextualism* (Lerner, 1986, 1991, in press; Lerner & Kauffman, 1985; Lerner & Miller, 1993; Miller & Lerner, 1994)—has emerged within land-grant institutions promoting this home economics vision of integrative, reciprocal, and dynamic relations among developing individuals, families, and contexts (cf. Featherman, 1983). This theory embeds the study of children in the actual families, neighborhoods, and communities within which they live their lives. Moreover, the model—when fully implemented—synthesizes research with policy and program design, delivery, and evaluation and involves both multiprofessional collaboration and full partnership with the communities within which science and service are being conducted (Lerner & Miller, 1993). In other words, the people whom science is intended to serve are full collaborators in the process of research and outreach.

This model may be of use in narrowing the above-noted gaps between research and the practical needs of our nation's diverse children, adolescents, and families. As such, I first provide some background to this perspective and then describe the model's synthetic approach to research and application.

2

An Overview of
Developmental Contextualism

Over the past two decades, the study of children and their families has evolved in at least three significant directions. These trends involve (a) changes in the conceptualization of the nature of the person, (b) the emergence of a life-span perspective about human development, and (c) stress on the contexts of development. These trends were both products and producers of developmental contextualism. This perspective has promoted a rationale for a synthesis of research and outreach, a synthesis focused on the diversity of children and on the contexts within which they develop.

Developmental contextualism stresses that bidirectional relations exist among the multiple levels of organization involved in human life (e.g., biology, psychology, social groups, and culture) (Bronfenbrenner, 1977, 1979; Lerner, 1986, 1991, in press). These dynamic relations provide a framework for the structure of human behavior (Ford & Lerner, 1992). In addition, this system is itself dynamically interactive with historical changes; this temporality provides a change component to human life (Dixon, Lerner, & Hultsch, 1991). In other words, within developmental contextualism, a changing configuration of relationships constitutes the basis of human life—of behavior and development (Ford & Lerner, 1992).

Developmental contextualism is a perspective about human development that takes an integrative approach to the multiple levels of organiza-

14

tion presumed to comprise the nature of human life, that is, *fused* (Tobach & Greenberg, 1984) *and changing relations* among biological, psychological, and social contextual levels comprise the process of developmental change. Rather than attempt to understand variables from these levels of analysis by either *reductionism* (conceptualizing the levels as all composed of common elements that function in the same way) or *parallel processing* (conceptualizing the levels as different, separate, and independent), the developmental contextual view rests on the idea that variables from these levels of analysis are dynamically interactive—they are reciprocally influential over the course of human ontogeny.

Within developmental contextualism, levels are conceived of as integrative organizations. That is,

> the concept of integrative levels recognizes as equally essential for the purpose of scientific analysis both the isolation of parts of a whole and their integration into the structure of the whole. It neither reduces phenomena of a higher level to those of a lower one, as in mechanism, or describes the higher level in vague nonmaterial terms which are but substitutes for understanding, as in vitalism. Unlike other "holistic" theories, it never leaves the firm ground of material reality. . . . The concept points to the need to study the organizational interrelationships of parts and whole. (Novikoff, 1945, p. 209)

Moreover, Tobach and Greenberg (1984) have stressed that

> the interdependence among levels is of great significance. The dialectic nature of the relationship among levels is one in which lower levels are subsumed in higher levels so that any particular level is an integration of preceding levels. . . . In the process of integration, or fusion, *new* levels with their own characteristics result. (p. 2; italics in original)

If the course of human development is the product of the processes involved in the fusions (or dynamic interactions) (Lerner, 1978, 1979, 1984) among integrative levels, then the processes of development are more plastic than often previously believed (cf. Brim & Kagan, 1980). Within this perspective, the context for development is not seen merely as a simple stimulus environment, but rather as an "ecological environment . . . conceived topologically as a nested arrangement of concentric structures, each contained within the next" (Bronfenbrenner, 1979, p. 22) and including variables from biological, psychological, physical, and sociocultural levels, all changing interdependently across history (Riegel, 1975, 1976a, 1976b).

The central idea in developmental contextualism is that changing, reciprocal relations (or dynamic interactions) between individuals and the multiple contexts within which they live comprise the essential process of human development (Lerner, 1986; Lerner & Kauffman, 1985). Accordingly, from a developmental contextual perspective, human behavior is both biological and social (Featherman & Lerner, 1985; Tobach & Schneirla, 1968). In fact, no form of life as we know it comes into existence independent of other life. No animal lives in total isolation from others of its species across its entire life span (Tobach, 1981; Tobach & Schneirla, 1968). Biological survival requires meeting the demands of the environment or, as I note later, attaining a *goodness of fit* (Chess & Thomas, 1984; Lerner & Lerner, 1983, 1989; Thomas & Chess, 1977) with the context. Because this environment is populated by other members of one's species, adjustment to (or fit with) these other organisms is a requirement of survival (Tobach & Schneirla, 1968).

Human evolution has promoted this link between biological and social functioning (Featherman & Lerner, 1985; Gould, 1977). Early humans were relatively defenseless, having neither sharp teeth nor claws. Coupled with the dangers of living in the open African savanna, where much of early human evolution occurred, group living was essential for survival (Masters, 1978; Washburn, 1961). Therefore, human beings were more likely to survive if they acted in concert with the group than if they acted in isolation. Human characteristics that support social relations (e.g., attachment, empathy) may have helped human survival over the course of its evolution (Hoffman, 1978; Hogan, Johnson, & Emler, 1978; Sahlins, 1978). Thus, for several reasons, humans at all portions of their life spans may be seen as embedded in a social context with which they have important relationships.

Much of the history of the study of human development prior to the mid-1970s was predicated on either organismic or mechanistic (reductionistic) models (Overton & Reese, 1973, 1981; Reese & Overton, 1970). In turn, it is accurate to say that, since the 1970s, developmental contextual conceptions have been increasingly prominent bases of scholarly advances in human development theory and methodology (Dixon & Lerner, 1992; Dixon et al., 1991; Lerner, Hultsch, & Dixon, 1983; Riegel, 1975, 1976a, 1976b; Sameroff, 1975, 1983). Indeed, the three above-noted themes in the study of human development define the place of developmental contextualism in theory and research over the past two decades. Accordingly, it is useful to discuss each of these themes in some detail.

CHILDREN'S INFLUENCES
ON THEIR OWN DEVELOPMENT

Children have come to be understood as active producers of their own development (Bell, 1968; Lerner & Spanier, 1978; Lewis & Rosenblum, 1974; Thomas, Chess, Birch, Hertzig, & Korn, 1963). These contributions primarily occur through the reciprocal relations individuals have with other significant people in their context: for example, children with family members, caregivers, teachers, and peers.

The content and functional significance of the influences that people have on others and, in turn, on themselves, occur in relation to people's characteristics of individuality (Schneirla, 1957). Individual differences in people evoke differential reactions in others, reactions that provide feedback to people and influence the individual character of their further development (Schneirla, 1957). Accordingly, individuality—diversity among people—is central in understanding the way in which any given person is an active agent in his or her own development (Lerner, 1982, 1991; Lerner & Busch-Rossnagel, 1981). In other words, diversity has core, substantive meaning and, as such, implications for all studies of human development.

To illustrate these points, it is useful to note that there is an old adage that the child is father to the man. This saying means simply that a person's characteristics when he or she is a child relate to his or her characteristics during adulthood. However, there is another way of interpreting this saying: How we behave and think as adults—and perhaps especially as parents—is very much influenced by our experiences with our children. Our children as much rear us as we do them. The very fact that we are parents makes us different adults than we would be if we were childless. But, more important, the specific and often special characteristics of a particular child influence us in unique ways. How we behave toward our children depends quite a lot on how they have influenced us to behave. Such child influences are termed *child effects*.

By influencing the parents that are influencing him or her, the child is shaping a source of his or her own development. In this sense, children are producers of their own development (Lerner, 1982), and the presence of such child effects constitutes the basis of *bidirectional* relations between parents and children. Of course, this bidirectional relation continues when the child is an adolescent and an adult. And corresponding relations exist between the person and siblings, friends, teachers, and indeed all other significant people in his or her life. Indeed, this child-other relation is the basic feature of the developmental contextual relations that characterize the social creature we call a human being. To elucidate this core relation it is useful to continue our emphasis on *child* effects (on person-context *relations* involving children), recognizing of course that we can readily extend other examples to include adolescents, adults, the aged, or the parents with whom the child interacts.

As noted above, child effects emerge largely as a consequence of a child's individual distinctiveness. All children, with the exception of genetically identical (monozygotic) twins, have a unique genotype, that is, a unique genetic inheritance. Similarly, no two children, including monozygotic twins, experience precisely the same environment. All human characteristics, be they behavioral or physical, arise from an interrelation of genes and environment (Anastasi, 1958; Lerner, 1986). Given the uniqueness of each child's genetic inheritance and environment, the distinctiveness of each child is assured (Feldman & Lewontin, 1975; Hirsch, 1970). In other words, every child is unique and therefore individually different from every other child.

Child individuality is represented diagrammatically in Figure 2.1 in respect to Child A (represented as a circle) and to Child B (represented as the bottom triangle). This individuality may be illustrated by drawing on the study of temperament (Chess & Thomas, 1984; Thomas & Chess, 1977; Thomas et al., 1963). Temperament is a characteristic of a child's behavior that describes *how* he or she acts. For instance, all children eat and sleep. Temperament is the *style* of eating or sleeping shown by the child; if the child eats the same amount at every meal and/or gets hungry at the same time, then this child has, in regard to eating, a regular, or rhythmic, temperament. A child who gets hungry at different times of the day or who may eat a lot or a little without any seeming predictability, would, in regard to eating, have an arrhythmic temperament. Similarly, obviously all children sleep. However, some children may sleep irregularly, that is, for seemingly unpredictable (at least to their parents) lengths of time, periods interspersed with wakeful periods of crying and fussing. Let

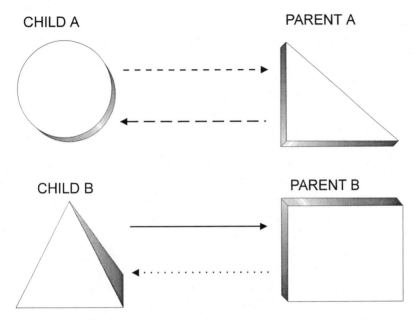

Figure 2.1. Parents' behaviors toward their children are related both to their own and to their children's characteristics of individuality.

us say Child A is like this; he or she is an arrhythmic eater and sleeper. Other children might sleep and eat in a more regularly patterned way, and/or when awake they may show more smiling than crying and fussing. Let this be Child B.

The importance of these individual differences arises when we recognize that as a consequence of their individuality, children will present different stimulation to parents. Child A and Child B present different stimuli to their parents as a consequence of their respective eating and sleep/wake patterns; the experience for a parent of having a pleasant, regularly sleeping child, who is predictable in regard to eating habits as well, is quite different from the experience for a parent who has a moody, irregularly sleeping and eating child. The different stimulation provided by Child A and Child B is also represented in Figure 2.1, by the small-dashed and solid-lined arrows going from Child A to Parent A and from Child B to Parent B, respectively.

The effect of the child's stimulation of the parent depends in part on the parent's own characteristics of individuality. However, to explain this point, it is useful to consider the second theme in the literature that helped crystallize the developmental contextual view of human development.

DEVELOPMENT AS A LIFE-SPAN PHENOMENON

The emergence of interest during the 1970s and 1980s in a life-span perspective about human development led to the understanding that development occurs in more than the childhood or adolescent years (Baltes, 1968, 1987; Block, 1971; Brim & Kagan, 1980; Elder, 1974, 1980; Featherman, 1983; Riley, 1979; Schaie, 1965). Parents as well as children develop as distinct individuals across life (Lerner & Spanier, 1978). Parents develop both as adults in general and, more specifically, in their familial and extra-familial (e.g., vocational or career) roles (Vondracek, Lerner, & Schulenberg, 1986). Indeed, the influence of a child on his or her parents will depend in part on the prior experience the adult has had with the parental role and on the other roles in which the parent is engaged (e.g., worker, adult-child, and caregiver for an aged parent) (Hetherington & Baltes, 1988). Thus a person's unique history of experiences and roles and his or her unique biological (e.g., genetic) characteristics combine to make that person unique—and with time, given the accumulation of the influences of distinct roles and experiences, increasingly more unique across the course of life (Lerner, 1988). This uniqueness is the basis of the specific feedback a parent gives to his or her individual child.

That is, parents who are stimulated differentially may be expected to differentially react to, or process (e.g., think and feel about), the stimulation provided by their child. Child A might evoke feelings of frustration and exasperation and thoughts of concern in his or her parents (Brazelton, Koslowski, & Main, 1974; Lewis & Rosenblum, 1974). And, especially among first-time parents, it is possible that parents might wonder if they will have the personal and marital resources to handle such a child (Chess & Thomas, 1984). We might expect, however, that the thoughts and feelings evoked in parents by Child B might be markedly different. Certainly, the parents of Child B would be better rested than Child A's parents. When their child was awake, they would have a child with a more regularly positive mood, and this too would present less stress on them as parents and as spouses. Figure 2.1 also illustrates the presence of different types of reactions by the parents of Child A and Child B. The individual reaction of

Parent A is represented as a right triangle, whereas the individuality of Parent B is represented as a rectangle.

The individuality of these parental reactions underscores the idea that parents are as individually distinct as are their children. Not all parents of an irregularly eating and sleeping, moody child will react with concern and/or frustration. Similarly, some parents will be stressed by even the most regular, predictable, and positive of children. Such parental individuality makes child effects more complicated to study. However, at the same time, parental individuality underscores the uniqueness of each child's context. Simply, then, it may be expected that as a consequence of the different stimulation received from their children, and in relation to their own characteristics of individuality, parents will provide differential feedback to their children.

Such differential feedback may take the form of different behavior shown to children by parents and/or of different emotional climates created in the home (Brazelton et al., 1974). For instance, the parents of Child A might take steps to alter his or her eating and sleep/wake patterns. In regard to sleeping, they might try to cut naps short during the day so that the child will be more tired in the evening. In addition, during the time when they are appraising the success of their attempts to put the child on an imposed schedule, a general sense of tenseness might pervade the household. "Will we have another sleepless night? Will we be too tired to be fully effective at work?" they might wonder.

In sum, then, Figure 2.1 also illustrates the presence of differential feedback by the parents of Child A and Child B (see the large-dashed and dotted arrows going from Parent A to Child A and from Parent B to Child B, respectively). This feedback becomes an important part of the child's experience, and this feedback is distinct in that it is based on the effect of the child's individuality on the parent. Thus the feedback serves to promote the child's individuality further.

Circular Functions and Bidirectional Socialization

The reciprocal child-parent relations involved in child effects constitute a circular function (Schneirla, 1957) in individual development: Children stimulate differential reactions in their parents, and these reactions provide the basis of feedback to the children, that is, return stimulation that influences their further individual development. These circular functions underscore the point that children (and adolescents and adults) are producers of their own development and that people's relations to their contexts involve bidirectional exchanges (Lerner, 1982; Lerner & Busch-Rossnagel, 1981). The parent shapes the child, but part of what determines the way in which the parent does this is the child himself or herself.

Children shape their parents—as adults, as spouses, and of course as parents per se—and in so doing children help organize feedback to themselves, feedback that contributes further to their individuality and thus starts the circular function all over again (that is, returns the child effects process to its first component). Characteristics of behavioral or personality individuality allow the child to contribute to this circular function. However, this idea of circular functions needs to be extended, that is, in and of itself the notion is mute regarding the specific characteristics of the feedback (e.g., its positive or negative valence) a child will receive as a consequence of his or her individuality. In other words, to account for the specific character of child-context relations, the circular functions model needs to be supplemented; this is the contribution of the goodness-of-fit model.

The Goodness-of-Fit Model

Just as a child brings his or her characteristics of individuality to a particular social setting, there are demands placed on the child by virtue of the social and physical components of the setting. These demands may take the form of (a) attitudes, values, or stereotypes that are held by others in the context regarding the person's attributes (either his or her physical or behavioral characteristics); (b) the attributes (usually behavioral) of others in the context with whom the child must coordinate, or fit, his or her attributes (also, in this case, usually behavioral) for adaptive interactions to exist; or (c) the physical characteristics of a setting (e.g., the presence or absence of access ramps for the motorically handicapped) that require the child to possess certain attributes (again, usually behavioral abilities) for the most efficient interaction within the setting to occur.

The child's individuality, in differentially meeting these demands, provides a basis for the specific feedback he or she gets from the socializing environment. For example, considering the demand domain of attitudes, values, or stereotypes, teachers and parents may have relatively individual and distinct expectations about behaviors desired of their students and children, respectively. Teachers may want students who show little distractibility, but parents might desire their children to be moderately distractible, for example, when they require their children to move from television watching to dinner or bed. Children whose behavioral individuality was either generally distractible or generally not distractible would thus differentially meet the demands of these two contexts. Problems of adjustment to school or home might thus develop as a consequence of a child's lack of match (or goodness of fit) in either or both settings.

Thomas and Chess (1977, 1980, 1981) and Lerner and Lerner (1983, 1989) have found that if a child's characteristics of individuality provide a goodness of fit (or match) with the demands of a particular setting, adaptive outcomes will accrue in that setting. Those children whose characteristics match most of the settings within which they exist receive supportive or positive feedback from the contexts and show evidence of the most adaptive behavioral development. In turn, of course, poorly fit or mismatched children, those whose characteristics are incongruent with one or most settings, appear to show alternative developmental outcomes.

In sum, then, the literatures on child effects and on the life-span perspective promote a concern with individual differences; variation in developmental pathways across life; and the developmental contextual idea that changing relations between the person and his or her context provide the basis, across life, of the individual's unique repertoire of physical, psychological, and behavioral characteristics (Lerner, 1991). The recognition of this link between person and context was a product and a producer of the third theme emerging in the study of human development since the 1970s.

DEVELOPMENT IN ITS ECOLOGICAL CONTEXT

The study of children and their parents became increasingly *contextualized,* or placed within the broader ecology of human development, during this period (Bronfenbrenner, 1977, 1979; Elder, 1974; Garbarino, 1992; Pepper, 1942). This focus has involved a concern with the real-life situations within which children and families exist. This focus has led also to the study of the bidirectional relations between the family and the other social settings within which children and parents function, for instance, the workplace, the welfare office, the day care, the Medicaid screening office, and the formal and the nonformal educational and recreational settings present in a neighborhood or a community (Lewis & Fiering, 1978; Lewis & Rosenblum, 1974).

To understand how the social context contributes to bidirectional person-context relations, we should reiterate that a child is *not* best thought of as merely similar to all other children or as simply different from others in respect to only one, or even just a few, characteristics. Instead, individual differences exist in respect to numerous characteristics. To illustrate, Figure 2.2 divides the child into components reflecting some of the several dimensions of individuality that exist. The slice labeled Etc. is used to indicate that there are numerous other characteristics of individuality that might be mentioned. The slice labeled Developmental Level is used to indicate that all of the child's characteristics of individuality change over time.

I have illustrated how at least some of these changes occur through the bidirectional relations the child has with his or her parents. However, what I have not illustrated to this point is that parents too are made up of multiple dimensions of individuality that, as with the child, develop across time (e.g., see Baltes, 1987). The multiple dimensions of the parent are also presented in Figure 2.2, along with arrows to indicate the bidirectional relations that exist between the child and his or her parent.

Another point not yet illustrated is that the parent-child relationship does not exist in isolation. Both the child and the parent have other social roles. These roles lead both children and parents into social relationships with other groups of people, that is, with other social networks. Parents are also spouses, adult children of their own parents, workers, and neighbors. Children also may be siblings and friends of other children, and as they progress through childhood and later adolescence, they become students and often at least part-time employees, respectively. The sorts of relationships in these other social networks in which children and parent engage when outside of their roles of child or parent, respectively, can be expected to influence the parent-child relationship (Bronfenbrenner, 1977, 1979).

A child's poor performance at school may influence his or her behavior in the home, and especially, may alter the quality of the parent-child relationship. In turn, a problematic home situation—as is experienced by children in families wherein parental abuse or neglect of the child occurs—will affect the child's relationships with peers, teachers, and other family members (Baca Zinn & Eitzen, 1993; Belsky, Lerner, & Spanier, 1984).

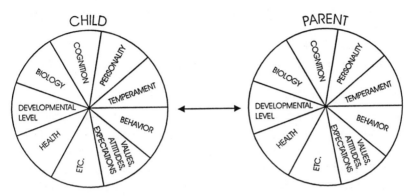

Figure 2.2. Multiple dimensions are also involved in the bidirectional relations between a child and a parent.

In regard to parents, strain in the spousal relationship can occur if the adult spends too much energy in his or her parental caregiving role (J. Lerner, 1994). For instance, a child's unpredictable sleep pattern and negative mood when awake can severely tax his or her parents' energy. Energy and time needed for parents to be good spouses to each other therefore may not be available. In addition, the fatigue caused by the demands of parental roles can be expected to influence parents' performance in the workplace (J. Lerner, 1994). It is difficult for people who have been up all night caring for a crying infant to be at their best at work the next morning. In turn, of course, problems at work can be brought home. Parents whose energies are significantly depleted outside the home may not have the stamina during the evening to be attentive, patient parents to their children (or attentive, emotionally supportive spouses for their mates).

Thus bidirectional relationships exist between the child and the parent (Bornstein & Tamis-LeMonda, 1990; Lerner & Lerner, 1987), and these relationships are in turn reciprocally related to the other social networks within which the dyad exists and to the broader societal and cultural context. For example, studying mother-infant dyads in the United States, France, and Japan, Bornstein et al. (1992) found both culture-general and culture-specific patterns of maternal responsiveness to characteristics of infant individuality (e.g., in regard to activity level, exploration, and vocalization). In short, then, the relationships among children, parents, and contexts constitute a complex state of affairs. One approach to the conceptualization of these relations that I see as particularly useful has been proposed by Urie Bronfenbrenner.

Bronfenbrenner's Model of the Ecology of Human Development

The contributions of Bronfenbrenner and his colleagues (e.g., Bronfenbrenner, 1979; Bronfenbrenner & Crouter, 1983; Garbarino, 1992) have been a major catalyst in promoting the contextualization of human development and in helping us understand why the study of development must move beyond its status during the 1970s as "the science of the strange behavior of children in strange situations with strange adults for the briefest possible periods of time" (Bronfenbrenner, 1977, p. 513). Bronfenbrenner (1977, 1979, 1983) has argued that human development needs to be understood as it occurs in its real-world setting or *ecology*. He believes that this ecology of human development is composed of four distinct, although interrelated, systems or types of settings.

The first, the *microsystem,* is composed of "the complex of relations between the developing person and environment in an immediate setting containing the person" (Bronfenbrenner, 1977, p. 515). For example, the family is the major microsystem for infant development in our society (Belsky et al., 1984); it involves interactions between the child, his or her parents, and any siblings that are present in the home. Other microsystems of infant life include the day care, nursery, or school setting, involving both child-teacher and child-peer interactions, and the playground, most often involving child-peer interactions.

An infant's microsystems may be interrelated. What occurs in day care may affect what happens in the family, and vice versa. Bronfenbrenner notes that such microsystem interrelations constitute a second ecological stratum termed the *mesosystem*. He defines it as "the interrelations among major settings containing the developing person at a particular point in his or her life" (Bronfenbrenner, 1977, p. 515).

Often, what happens in a microsystem (e.g., in an interaction between a child and a parent within the family context) may be influenced by events that occur in systems in which the child takes no part. For example, an adult who is a parent also has other social roles, for instance, as a worker. The child is probably not part of his or her parents' workplace interactions, but events that affect the parents at work can influence how they treat the child. If a parent has a particularly bad or tiring day at work, he or she may respond to the child more severely than otherwise for some disapproved act. Thus, because the people with whom the child lives inter-act in—are affected by—contexts other than those containing the child, the child may be affected by settings in which he or she plays no direct role. Bronfenbrenner sees such influences as constituting a third system within the ecology of human development. He labels it the *exosystem* and defines it as "an extension of the mesosystem embracing . . . specific social struc-tures, both formal and informal, that do not themselves contain the devel-oping person but impinge upon or encompass the immediate setting in which the person is found, and thereby delimit, influence, or even deter-mine what goes on there" (Bronfenbrenner, 1977, p. 515).

Finally, Bronfenbrenner notes that there exists a *macrosystem* within the ecology of human development. This system is composed of cultural values and beliefs as well as historical events (e.g., wars, floods, famines), both of which may affect the other ecological systems. For instance, natu-ral disasters may destroy the homes, schools, or other microsystems of a person or a group of developing people, and/or they may make certain necessities of life (e.g., food, fresh water) less available. In turn, cultural values influence the developing child in many ways. For example, cultural beliefs about the appropriateness of breastfeeding and about when wean-ing from the breast should occur can affect not only the nutritional status of infants but also their health status because mother's milk may make some children less likely to develop allergies later in life.

In short, then, Bronfenbrenner's model of the ecology of human devel-opment allows us to devise a means to represent the idea that the bidirec-tional socialization that occurs between children and parents is embedded in a still more complex system of social networks and of societal, cultural, and historical influences.

Levels of Embeddedness

The core idea in developmental contextualism is that the organism (or-ganismic attributes or, most generally, biology) and context cannot be separated (Gottlieb, 1991, 1992; Lerner, 1984; Tobach, 1981). Both are fused across all of life and thus across history. One way to begin to illus-trate just what is involved in this relation, even for one person, is to con-sider the diagram presented in Figure 2.3 (see Lerner, 1984, 1986). Here I continue to use the representations introduced in Figure 2.2 to represent an individual child and parent. As before, the mutual influence between child and parent, their fusion with each other, is represented in the figure by the bidirectional arrows between them.

It is important to indicate at this point that we may speak of dynamic interactions between parent and child that pertain to either social or physical (for instance, biological or physiological) relations. For example, in regard to social relationships, the parent demands attention from the child, but the child does not show it; this "lights" the parent's short fuse of tolerance; he or she scolds the child, who then cries; this creates remorse in the parent and elicits soothing behaviors from him or her; the child is calmed, snuggles up to the parent, and now both parties in the relationship show positive emotions and are happy (see Tubman & Lerner, 1994, for data pertinent to such parent-child relationships).

In turn, I may also illustrate dynamic interactions that involve not only the exchange of "external" social behaviors but involve as well biological or physiological processes. For example, parental religious practices, rearing practices, or financial status may influence the child's diet and nutritional status, health, and medical care. In turn, the contraction of an infectious disease by either parent or child can lead to the other member of the relationship contracting the disease. Moreover, the health and physical status of the child influences the parent's own feelings of well-being and his or her hopes and aspirations regarding the child (Finkelstein, 1993).

Thus the child's physiological status and development are not disconnected from his or her behavioral and social context (in this example, parental) functioning, and development (e.g., see Finkelstein, 1993; Ford & Lerner, 1992; Howard, 1978). The inner and outer worlds of the child are fused and dynamically interactive. In addition, of course, the same may be said of the parent and, in fact, of the parent-child relationship. Each of these foci—child, parent, or relationship—is part of a larger, enmeshed system of fused relations among the multiple levels that comprise the ecology of human life (Bronfenbrenner, 1979).

For instance, illustrated in Figure 2.3 is the idea that both parent and child are embedded in a broader social network and that each person has reciprocal reactions with this network. This set of relations occurs because both the child and the parent are much more than just people playing only one role in life. As already emphasized, the child may also be a sibling, a

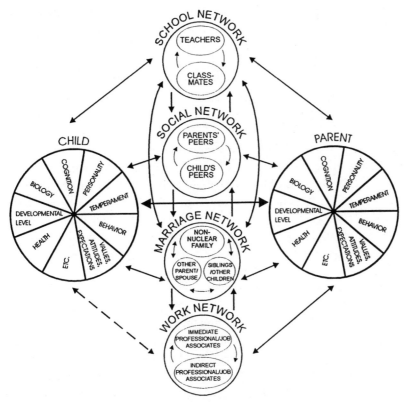

Figure 2.3. Parent-child relations are influenced by the interpersonal and institutional networks within which parents and children are embedded.

peer, and a student; the parent may also be a spouse, a worker, and an adult child. All of these networks of relations are embedded within a particular community, society, and culture. And, finally, all of these relations are continually changing across time, across history. Simply, for all portions of the system of person-context, or biology-environment, relations envisioned in developmental contextualism, change across time is an integral, indeed inescapable, feature of human life.

Thus Figure 2.3 illustrates that within and among each of the networks that is depicted one may conceive of bidirectional relationships existing among the people populating the network. A child effect may function, in a sense, like a small pebble thrown into a quiet lake. It can prompt a large ripple. In turn, of course, the reverse of this possibility can occur. Events in settings lying far beyond the child-parent relationship can influence it. For instance, the resources in a community for child day care during the parent's working hours, the laws (e.g., regarding tax exemptions) or social programs available in a society supporting day care, and the cultural values regarding families who place their infants in day care all exert an impact on the quality of the parent-child relationship.

Moreover, as I have just noted, the child-parent relationship, and the social networks in which it is located, are embedded in still larger community, societal, cultural, and historical levels of organization. These relations are illustrated in Figure 2.4. Time—history—cuts through all the systems. This feature of the figure is introduced to remind us that, as with the people populating these social systems, change is always occurring. Diversity within time is created as change across time (across history) introduces variation into all the levels of organization involved in the system depicted in Figure 2.4.

In other words, people develop and the family changes from one having infants and young children to one having teenagers to an empty nest: The children have left the home of their parents to live elsewhere and very likely to start their own families. Similarly, communities, societies, and cultures change too (Elder, 1974; Elder, Modell, & Parke, 1993; Garbarino, 1992; Hernandez, 1993). In addition, each of these multiple levels is embedded in the natural and human-designed physical ecology, a physical world that, of course, changes also. Changes at one or more of these levels produce changes in the other levels as well, given their bidirectional connections.

Finally, as I have noted, all changes are embedded in history (Baltes, 1987; Elder, 1974; Elder et al., 1993); that is, time cuts through all levels of organization. As such, the nature of parent-child relations, family life and development, and societal and cultural influences on the child-parent-family system are influenced by both *normative* and *nonnormative* historical changes (Baltes, 1987) or, in other words, by evolutionary (i.e., gradual) and revolutionary (i.e., abrupt) (Werner, 1957) historical changes. This system of multiple, interconnected, or fused (Tobach & Greenberg, 1984) levels comprises a complete depiction of the integrated organization involved in the developmental contextual view of human development (Lerner, 1986, 1991).

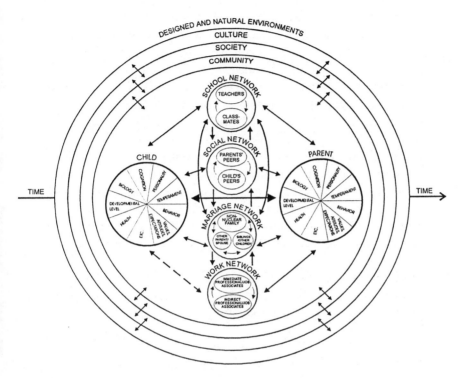

Figure 2.4. The developmental contextual view of human development: Parent-child relations and interpersonal and institutional networks are embedded in and influenced by particular community, societal, cultural, and designed and natural environments, all changing across time (across history).

IMPLICATIONS FOR RESEARCH AND APPLICATION

In essence, (a) individuality (diversity); (b) change, involving both the individual and the context; and, as a consequence, (c) further individuality are the essential features of human development within developmental contextualism. Given that the multiple levels of change involved in person-context relations may involve individuals at any point in their lives, whether they are infants or young children, on the one hand, or adults (and acting in roles such as parents, spouses, or teachers), on the other, it is possible to see why a developmental contextual perspective provides a useful frame for studying development across the life span.

The possibility that bidirectional relations exist across the life span among all the levels shown in Figure 2.4 represents a formidable state of complexity, which behavioral and social science theory and research must address. If scholarship does not cope with this complexity, then neither research nor application will be adequate. That is, research inattentive to the complexity of person-context relations will be deficient in that either it will fail to appreciate the substantive nature of individual, familial, or relationship variation, and/or it will mistakenly construe variation around some (potentially specifically inapplicable) mean level as, at best, error variance, that is, differences that are random and nonmeaningful (Lerner, 1991, in press). In turn, applications—policies and/or programs (that are at least ideally) derived from research (Lerner & Miller, 1993)—will be insufficiently fit with the needs of the specific people intended to be served by these interventions, *if* it is the case that these activities are insufficiently informed by knowledge about the specific characteristics of individuality of these groups.

However, developmental contextualism offers an alternative to this situation. It does so by stressing the importance of a focus on diversity and context for integrated research and outreach.

3

An Integrative Vision of Human Development Research and Outreach

Developmental contextualism emphasizes the bidirectional connections between the individual and the actual (ecologically valid) settings within which he or she lives. This emphasis has brought to the fore of concern in the social and behavioral sciences both *diversity* (individual differences) and *context* (of peoples and their sociocultural institutions). In addition, developmental contextualism stresses the relation between the individual and his or her context. This stress has resulted in the recognition that a synthesis of perspectives from multiple disciplines is needed to understand the multilevel (e.g., person, family, and community) integrations involved in human development. Furthermore, there has been a recognition that to understand the basic process of human development—the process involved in the changing relations between individuals and contexts—both descriptive and explanatory research must be conducted within the actual ecology of people's lives.

Descriptive research involves the depiction, or representation, of development as it exists for a given person or group, in one or more contexts, at one or more points in time. Explanatory research involves the introduction (through manipulation or statistical modeling) of variation into such person-context relations. These planned variations in the course of human life are predicated on (a) theoretical ideas about the source of particular developmental phenomena (for specific combinations of people

33

and contexts) or (b) theoretically guided interests about the extent to which a particular developmental phenomenon (e.g., cognitive development in the aged years) may show systematic change in structure and/or function, that is, *plasticity,* across the life span (Baltes, 1987; Lerner, 1984). In the case of either a or b, such researcher-introduced variation is an attempt to simulate the natural variation of life; if theoretical expectations are confirmed, the outcomes of such investigations provide an explanation of how developmental change occurs within a person or group.

Given the developmental contextual focus on studying person-context relations within the actual ecology of human development, *explanatory investigations by their very nature constitute intervention research.* In other words, the goal of developmental contextual explanatory research is to understand the ways in which variations in ecologically valid person-context relations account for the character of actual or potential trajectories of human development, that is, life paths enacted in the natural laboratory of the real world. Therefore, to gain understanding of how theoretically relevant variations in such person-context relations may influence actual or to-be-actualized developmental trajectories, the researcher may introduce policies and/or programs as, if you will, experimental manipulations of the proximal and/or distal natural ecology. Evaluations of the outcomes of such interventions become, then, a means to bring data to bear on theoretical issues pertinent to changing person-context relations and, more specifically, to the plasticity in human development that may exist, or that may be capitalized on, to enhance human life (Lerner, 1988). In other words, a key theoretical issue for explanatory research in human development is the extent to which changes—in the multiple, fused levels of organization comprising human life—can alter the structure and/or function of behavior and development.

Of course, independent of any researcher-imposed attempts to intervene in the course of human development, the naturally occurring events experienced by people constantly shape, texture, and help direct the course of their lives. That is, the accumulation of the specific roles and events a person experiences across life—involving normative age-graded events, normative history-graded events, and nonnormative events (Baltes, 1987; Baltes, Reese, & Lipsitt, 1980)—alters each person's developmental trajectory in a manner that would not have occurred had another set of roles and events been experienced. The between-person differences in within-person change that exist as a consequence of these naturally occurring experiences attest to the magnitude of the systematic changes in structure and function—the plasticity—that characterizes human life (Lerner, 1984).

Explanatory research is necessary, however, to understand what variables, from what levels of organization, are involved in particular instances of plasticity that have been seen to exist. In addition, such research is necessary to determine what instances of plasticity may be created by science or society. In other words, explanatory research is needed to ascertain the extent of human plasticity or, in turn, the limits of plasticity (Lerner, 1984). From a developmental contextual perspective, the conduct of such research requires the scientist to alter the natural ecology of the person or group he or she is studying. Such research may involve either proximal and/or distal variations in the context of human development (Lerner & Ryff, 1978), but, in any case, these manipulations constitute theoretically guided alterations of the roles and events a person or group experiences at, or over, a portion of the life span.

These alterations are indeed, then, interventions: They are planned attempts to alter the system of person-context relations constituting the basic process of change; they are conducted to ascertain the specific bases or to test the limits of particular instances of human plasticity (Baltes, Dittmann-Kohli, & Dixon, 1984; Baltes, Smith, & Staudinger, 1992). These interventions are a researcher's attempt to substitute designed person-context relations for naturally occurring ones, a substitution done in an attempt to understand the process of changing person-context relations providing the basis of human development. In short, then, basic research in human development is intervention research.

Accordingly, the cutting edge of theory and research in human development lies in the application of the conceptual and methodological expertise of human development scientists to the natural ontogenetic laboratory of the real world. Multilevel, and hence qualitatively and quantitatively multivariate, and longitudinal research methods must be used by scholars from multiple disciplines to derive, from theoretical models of person-context relations, programs of research that involve the design, delivery, and evaluation of interventions aimed at enhancing—through scientist-introduced variation—the course of human development.

A similar argument has been made by Lanier (1990) in regard to how past approaches to educational research must be altered to improve teaching and the educational development of youth. Calling for what she terms *interventionist inquiry* (Lanier, 1990), Lanier argues for educational research on teaching that is comparable to that which Dewey supported in his Chicago years—i.e., (1) experimentation within a naturalistic setting, notably the laboratory school; (2) a testing ground and link between scientific and social innovation; and (3) a means to increase educational efficiency by creating a more cohesive, interrelated social system, education being an interactive process among schools and various other social institutions. . . . In order to have the best chance of improving practice, scholarly inquiry needs to occur in conjunction with substantial ongoing development and responsible experimentation in schools. . . . This is why it is essential to combine rigorous inquiry with intervention on a systemic basis. (pp. 1-2)

In short, in developmental contextualism there is a stress on ontological (and on epistemological, I would add) relationism and contextualization. These emphases have brought to the fore of scientific, intervention, and policy concerns issues pertinent to the functional importance of diverse person-context interactions. Examples are studies of the effects of variations in maternal employment on infant, child, and young adolescent development; the importance of differences in quality day care for the immediate and long-term development in children of healthy physical, psychological, and social characteristics; and the effects of variations in marital role strain and in marital stability-instability on the healthy development of children and adolescents.

A FOCUS ON DIVERSITY

As greater study has been made of the actual contexts within which people live, behavioral and social scientists have shown increasing appreciation of the diversity of patterns of individual and family development that exist and that comprise the range of human structural and functional characteristics. Such diversity—involving racial, ethnic, gender, physical handicap, national, and cultural variation—has, to the detriment of the knowledge base in human development, not been a prime concern of empirical analysis (Fisher & Brennan, 1992; Hagen et al., 1990).

For instance, Hagen et al. (1990) report the results of analyses of the content of articles published from 1930 through 1990 in *Child Development*, the flagship journal of the Society for Research in Child Development and, arguably, the most prestigious publication outlet for scientific scholarship about children. The Hagen et al. analyses indicate that across the more than half century since it began publication (in 1930) there has been little attention paid in the pages of *Child Development* either to diversity of people or to variation in their contexts.

Indeed, during the 1930 to 1990 period, only a very small proportion of the articles published in *Child Development* focused on the context of the child, and this proportion has continued to decrease. That is, between 1930 and 1969, the percentage of articles that had as a measurement focus only the child varied from between about 80% to 90%; however, between 1970 and 1990, the percentage was about 95% or more. In turn, between 1930 and 1964, the percentage of articles that had as a measurement focus the environment, or context, of child development varied from between about 10% to 15%; however, between 1969 and 1990, the percentage varied from about 2% to 0%. Obviously, then, with this low percentage of articles involving the measurement of context, the percentage of studies involving the measurement of child-context *relations,* that is, the focal unit of analysis stressed in developmental contextualism (Lerner, 1991), would be even lower.

And who was the child focused on in the research reported in the pages of *Child Development?* Was the absence of attention to the context of child development, an omission that therefore precluded any focus on the role of contextual variation (diversity) in children's development, associated with concern with the individual differences (diversity) that existed among the children participating in the research reported in the journal? Unfortunately, the answer to this question is no.

According to the analyses of Hagen et al. (1990), the participants in the studies published in *Child Development* were either middle-class, European American children or were children whose racial and socioeconomic status was not even mentioned by the authors of the articles published in the journal. For example, considering only the most recently completed 1980-1989 decade, about 50% of all articles did not specify the socioeconomic status of the children who were studied, and if socioeconomic status was noted, over 30% of the articles studied children from the middle class. In turn, in the 1980-1984 period, about 55% of all studies published in *Child Development* did not specify the race of the children participating in the research. In the period between 1984 and 1989, this percentage *increased* to about 65%. Moreover, in the minority of articles wherein race of participants was indicated, most articles reported studying

European American children: In the 1980-1984 period, about 29% of the articles studied these children, and in the 1984-1989 period, about 25% of the articles studied European American children.

It is important to note that this omission of concern with diversity was not just a characteristic of articles published in *Child Development*. To illustrate, Graham (1992) assessed the proportion of articles about African Americans published between 1970 and 1989 in the four major journals of the American Psychological Association that pertain to human behavior and development: the *Journal of Personality and Social Psychology*, the *Journal of Educational Psychology*, the *Journal of Consulting and Clinical Psychology*, and *Developmental Psychology*. Across these four journals, only about 5.5% of the articles published in the 1970-1974 period pertained to African Americans. And by the end of the 20-year period assessed by Graham (1992), that is, across the final 5 years within this period—between 1985 and 1989—the percentage of articles about African Americans published across the four journals *decreased* to about 1.5%.

Thus researchers publishing in the best disciplinary and multidisciplinary journals pertinent to research about child behavior and development appear to be increasingly less concerned about studying the diversity of people that comprise the youth of America. In other words, scholars publishing in the best journals in the field of human behavior and development have as a group acted either as if (a) they were studying the "generic child," a child whose individual and contextual characteristics were of such little importance that even mention of some of the relatively easily accessible instances of these characteristics (e.g., race and/or socioeconomic status) was not necessary, or as if (b) the only characteristics worth mentioning were European American, middle-class ones.

It may be deemed by some as impolite or impolitic to note this shortcoming of scientific inquiry. However, such lack of sensitivity to human individual and contextual diversity cannot continue: The absence of sensitivity to diversity is, clearly, morally repugnant to many people and, at least equally important in this context, such lack of sensitivity is simply bad science (Lerner, 1991, in press).

That is, from a developmental contextual perspective, there are several reasons why diversity should become a key focus of concern in the study of human development (Lerner, 1991, 1992, in press). As noted by McLoyd (1994), by 1990 about 25% of all Americans had African, Asian, Latino, or Native American ancestry. Moreover, the proportion of Americans from other than European backgrounds will continue to grow; for example, more than 80% of legal immigrants to America continue to be from non-European backgrounds (Barringer, 1991). Furthermore, McLoyd (1994) notes that higher fertility rates among minority groups continue to contribute to the increasing proportion of the American population that is comprised by groups that are now considered minorities. However, by the end of this century, the Latino population in America will increase by about 21%, the Asian American population by about 22%, and the African American population by about 12%; however, the European American population will grow by only about 2% (Barringer, 1991; McLoyd, 1994; Wetzel, 1987). Accordingly, by about the year 2000, approximately 33% of all American children and adolescents will be from "minority" groups, and in some states (e.g., California, Texas, and New Mexico) the majority of youth are already, or by the year 2000 will be, from minority groups (Dryfoos, 1990; Henry, 1990; McLoyd, 1994).

Given these demographic trends, it is not appropriate—and, in fact, it might be disastrous for the future health and welfare of America—to ignore in our scientific research or outreach the diversity of America's children. As stressed by McLoyd (1994):

> In view of these demographic changes, rendering minority children virtually invisible in the annals of knowledge about the conditions that facilitate and disrupt development is indefensible ethically. That some of the most pressing problems now facing America affect, disproportionately, children and youth from ethnic minority backgrounds makes it all the more so. It is also inimical to the long-term self-interests of the nation because minority youth's fraction of the total youth population is increasing precisely at a time when the proportion of youth in the total population is dwindling. . . . Consequently, the proportion of youths in the total population will continue to fall, reaching a low of 13% in 1996, down from 19% in 1980. The implications of this trend are far-reaching. The decline in the number of youth, and ultimately, the number of entrants into the labor force, means that the ratio of workers to retirees will shrink. The economic well-being of the nation will depend even more than at present on its ability to enhance the intellectual and social skills of all its youth, as these will be crucial for maximum productivity in the workplace. (pp. 59-60)

Moreover, evidence for the presence and substantive and societal importance of individual diversity is coupled with similar information relevant to the significance of contextual variation in human development. Consider first the nature of contemporary and historical diversity in the structure and function of the American family.

Diversity in the American Family

What sorts of family relations do we find in contemporary America? How are these comparable to those that existed in prior decades? I grew up at a time when the stereotypic American family was an intact nuclear one, with two biological parents and two or three children (named either David and Ricky, or Bud, Kitten, and Princess, respectively). Yet today, only one in five married couples with children fits this still popular stereotype of living in what has been termed the *Ozzie and Harriet* family, that is, the intact, never divorced, two-parent-two-child family wherein the father is the breadwinner and the mother is the homemaker (Ahlburg & De Vita, 1992; Hernandez, 1993). Indeed, as shown in Table 3.1, at any one time children and parents may live in several quite different family contexts (see Allison, 1993).

Moreover, the number of children living in many of the types of family contexts shown in Table 3.1 has increased dramatically in recent years. As an example, consider the category of foster care homes. Between 1987 and 1991, the number of children in foster care increased by more than 50%, from 300,000 to 460,000 (Carnegie Corporation of New York, 1994). Infants less than 12 months old are among the age groups of children most likely to be placed in such care (Carnegie Corporation of New York, 1994).

In addition, the cross-sectional location of people in one of the family contexts noted in Table 3.1 is complicated by the fact that such settings may change longitudinally over the course of the lives of children and parents and thus across generations (i.e., across history). This observation raises the need for a historically embedded developmental demographics of child-parent relations (Allison, 1993), a point underscored by the research of Featherman, Spenner, and Tsunematsu (1988) and, more recently, Hernandez (1993). For instance, Featherman et al. demonstrate that even with a contextual variable as seemingly general (and presumably somewhat stable) as social class, only approximately 46% of American children remain at age 6 in the social class within which they were born. Indeed, about 22% of all children born in the United States change from their initial social class during their *first year of life*. Moreover, during the

TABLE 3.1   Contemporary Family Contexts of Children and Youth

Intact nuclear (and biological)
Single parent (biological)
Intact nuclear (adoptive)
Single parent (adoptive)
Intact (blended)
    Heterosexual, homosexual
Single parent (step)
Intergenerational
Extended, without parent (e.g., child-aunt)
In loco parentis families/institutions
    Foster care homes
    Group homes
    Psychiatric hospitals
    Residential treatment facilities
    Juvenile detention facilities
Runaways
Street children/youth (e.g., adolescent prostitutes)
Homeless children

first 6 years of life, about 54% of American children have lived in two or more social classes (Featherman et al., 1988). Given the fact that social class structures the large majority of the resources and cultural values influencing families, these magnitudes of change underscore the need to appraise the diversity of child-family relations longitudinally (historically) as well as cross-sectionally.

This viewpoint is brought to the fore by the scholarship of Hernandez (1993). Using census and survey data, Hernandez (1993) describes several quite profound changes that have characterized the life courses of America's children and their families over the past 50 to 150 years. Adopting a perspective consonant with the stress in developmental contextualism on integrated relations between people and the multiple levels of the context within which they live, Hernandez argues that a person's life trajectory is constituted by, and differentiated from, those of others on the basis of (a) the specific order, duration, and timing of the particular events and resources experienced in life and (b) the number, characteristics, and activities of the family members with whom the person lives. Using this viewpoint as a frame, Hernandez describes what he labels as eight *revolutions* in the lives of America's children across this century.

Disappearance of the Two-Parent Farm
Family and the Growth of the One-Parent Family

Hernandez (1993) notes that between the late 18th century to almost the end of the 19th century the majority of American children between the ages of birth to 17 years lived in two-parent farm families. At the beginning of the 20th century, about 40% of all children in this age range still lived in such family settings, with slightly more than an additional 40% living in nonfarm, two-parent families with the father as the breadwinner and the mother as the homemaker. The remaining children in this age range at the beginning of this century (slightly more than 10%) lived either in dual-earner nonfarm or one-parent families or in no-parent situations.

By 1950, only about 15% of American children lived, during their first 17 years of life, in two-parent farm families, whereas almost 60% of American children in this age range lived in intact, nonfarm families wherein the father was the breadwinner and the mother was the homemaker. Dual-earner nonfarm or one-parent families were the settings wherein most of the remaining American children within this age range lived.

In 1990, however, fewer than 5% of America's children lived, during the first 17 years of their lives, in two-parent farm families. Moreover, fewer than 30% of children in this age range lived in intact nonfarm families wherein the father was the breadwinner and the mother was the homemaker. Rather, about 70% of all American children in this age range lived either in dual-earner nonfarm families or in one-parent families. Indeed, approximately 25% lived in one-parent families. In this regard, Hamburg (1992) observes that

> it is startling to realize that today most American children spend part of their childhood in a single-parent family. By age sixteen, close to half the children of married parents will see their parents divorce. Usually the child remains with the mother. For nearly half of these children, it will be five years or more before their mothers remarry. Close to half of all white children whose parents remarry will see the second marriage dissolve during their adolescence. Black women not only marry less often and experience more marital disruption, but also remarry more slowly and less often than white women. America exhibits a revolving-door pattern in marriage that is certainly stressful for developing children and adolescents. (p. 33)

Furthermore, the increase in one-parent families was coupled with a decrease across this century in the presence of a grandparent in the home. By 1990, about 80% of children in one-parent families did not live with a grandparent (U.S. Department of Commerce, 1991). Thus the parenting resources accruing from having two adults in the home are generally absent in contemporary American one-parent families; in the majority of such families there is no grandparent present to replace the resources represented by the absent parent.

Decrease in the Number of Siblings in the Family

In 1890, 46% of America's children lived in families wherein they had eight or more siblings. An additional 30% lived in families wherein they had between five and seven siblings, and 16% lived in families where they had either three or four siblings. Only 7% of America's children lived in families having either one or two siblings (Hernandez, 1993).

By 1940, however, families wherein a child had eight or more siblings accounted for only 10% of America's families. In turn, the percentages of American families wherein a child had either between five and seven siblings, three or four siblings, or only one or two siblings were 21%, 38%, and 30%, respectively (Hernandez, 1993).

In 1990, however, only 1% of America's children lived in families wherein they had eight or more siblings. In addition, only 5% of America's children lived in families with five to seven siblings, and about an additional 38% lived in families wherein they had either three or four siblings. In turn, about 57% lived in families with either one or two siblings (Hernandez, 1993).

This change in the number of siblings in the home has been coupled with a corresponding decrease in the average size of households in America. Indeed, Hamburg (1992) notes that the size of the average American household has diminished to its smallest level ever. In addition,

one-quarter of the nation's households consist of people living alone. This is twenty-three million individuals. The change has come rapidly. The number of people living alone more than doubled between 1970 and 1990—yet another indication of the dramatic transformation of American families taking place in recent decades. While this finding has positive as well as negative implications, it certainly highlights a major challenge to the adequacy of social supports under the transforming conditions of contemporary life. (Hamburg, 1992, pp. 12-13)

Increase in Parents' Education

Although years of school attendance and/or school completion rates are not necessarily good indexes of attained knowledge or of quality of education, there are considerable data indicating that the number of years of completed education by American children's parents has increased substantially. Hernandez (1993) reports that in the 1920s, about 60% of the children in America had fathers with at least 8 years of schooling, and about 15% of America's children had fathers with at least 4 years of high school education; the corresponding rates for mothers were a few percentage points higher than those for fathers.

In the 1950s, parental educational attainment had markedly increased. Approximately 90% of all mothers and about 87% of all fathers had 8 or more years of schooling. In turn, 60% of mothers and about 55% of fathers had at least 4 years of high school (Hernandez, 1993).

To the end of the 1980s, these trends of increasing parental education continued. By that time, about 96% of all mothers and fathers had 8 or more years of schooling. Moreover, about 80% of all mothers and about 85% of all fathers had at least 4 years of high school (Hernandez, 1993).

Growth of Mothers in the Labor Force

In 1900, only about 6% of the married women in America worked for wages (Hamburg, 1992). However, as documented by Hernandez (1993) and by J. Lerner (1994), the percentage of children with mothers in the labor force has increased dramatically across the past half century. Indeed, in 1940, only 10% of America's children had mothers in the labor force. In 1950, this percentage had only grown to 16%. However, in 1960, more than one quarter (26%) of America's children had mothers working outside the home, and by 1970, this proportion had grown to greater than one third (36%). In 1980, 49% of America's children had mothers in the labor force, and by 1990, this figure had grown to 59% (Hernandez, 1993). In two-parent families, about 67% of mothers are in the labor force (J. Lerner, 1994).

As noted by Hamburg (1992) and by J. Lerner (1994), this increase in maternal employment impacts on child and adolescent development in as yet incompletely understood or documented ways. For example, Hamburg (1992) notes that

> as women have opened up unprecedented opportunities for themselves and are making an enormous contribution to the well-being of the economy and the society, they have less time for their children. By and large, fathers and grandparents simply are not compensating for this historical shift.
>
> So families are living in a time of flux. It is a time of magnificent opportunities and of insidious stress. Just as the economic functions of the family moved out of the home early in the Industrial Revolution, so child-care functions, too, are now moving outside the home to a large extent. The child's development is less and less under parents' and grandparents' direct supervision and increasingly placed in the hands of strangers and near-strangers. In the main, this transformation was unforeseen and unplanned, and it is still poorly understood. (pp. 10-11)

One of the unplanned features of this transformation is that, in 1994, more than 5 million American children under 3 years of age were in the care of other adults when their parent or parents were at work. As noted by the Carnegie Corporation of New York (1994), much of the care received by these young children is of poor quality.

Changes in Fathers' Full-Time Employment

The marked growth in maternal employment since 1940 has been coupled with the fact that between the 1940s and the 1980s many of America's children lived with fathers who were not employed full time year round (Hernandez, 1993). In 1940, 40% of America's children lived with fathers who did not have full-time employment all year. In 1950, this rate fell to 32%, and by 1980, it fell still further to 24%.

However, between 1950 and 1980, the 8% decrease in children living with fathers who did not have full-time employment was offset by an 8% increase in children who did not have a father in the home (Hernandez, 1993). Given the percentage of American children that lived in such father-absent homes during this period, a phenomenon that will be discussed below, Hernandez (1993) notes that from the 1950s to the 1980s only about 60% of America's children lived with fathers who worked full time all of the year.

Growth of Single-Parent, Female-Head-of-Household Families

As noted above, during the past half century, there has been a dramatic increase in the percentage of American children living with only their mothers (Hernandez, 1993). In 1940, 1950, and 1960, the proportion of children living in single-parent, female-head-of-household families remained relatively steady, with 6.7%, 6.4%, and 7.7%, respectively, of children living in such households. However, between 1960 and 1990, the percentage of children living in such families almost tripled. In 1970 the percentage was 11.8%, in 1980 it was 16.2%, and in 1990 it was 20% (Hernandez, 1993).

In addition to out-of-wedlock births, a major reason for the growth of single-parent, female-head-of-household families is the rising rates of divorce in America. As noted by the Carnegie Corporation of New York (1994), in 1906, less than 1% of children per year experienced the divorce of their parents. However, by 1993, almost 50% of all children could expect to experience the divorce of their parents; on the average these children live 5 years in a single-parent family.

Disappearance of the Ozzie-and-Harriet Family

I noted above that over the course of the 20th century America has experienced a disappearance of the stereotypically predominant intact, two-parent family, wherein the father is the breadwinner, the mother is the homemaker, and two to three children either spend their lives in socioeconomic and personal security or are faced with problems that require only about 30 minutes (the time of the typical American television situation comedy) to resolve.

Hamburg (1992) notes that until the beginning of the 1960s most of the people in the United States believed that much of this stereotype was, in fact, true. Specifically, Hamburg (1992) indicates that Americans believed:

1. A family consists of a husband and wife living together with their children.
2. The father is the head of the family and should earn the family's income and give his name to his wife and children.
3. The mother's main tasks are to support and facilitate the work of her husband, guide her children's development, look after the home, and set a moral tone for the family.

4. Marriage is an enduring obligation for better and worse; the husband and wife have the joint task of coping with stresses, including those of the child's development; and sexual activity, especially by women, should be kept within the marriage.

5. Parents have an overriding responsibility for the well-being of their children during their early years; until they enter school, the parents have almost sole responsibility and even later must be the primary guardians of their children's education and discipline. (p. 32)

Although Hamburg (1992) stresses that Americans were aware that these beliefs were not necessarily readily actualized, the beliefs nevertheless represented ideals against which people's actual family lives were compared. However, Hernandez (1993) demonstrates that not only are such stereotypic family milieus largely absent in America—making the formerly held beliefs about the family difficult to maintain—but, since the 1940s, a decreasing minority of children have been born into such stereotyped families.

In 1940, 1950, 1960, and 1970, the percentage of children born into Ozzie-and-Harriet type families was 40.8%, 44.5%, 43.1%, and 37.3%, respectively. However, by 1980, this percentage fell to 27.4% (Hernandez, 1993). Moreover, few Americans spend their entire childhood and adolescent years in such family settings. Indeed, in 1920, only 31% of children and adolescents lived their first 17 years in these types of families; this percentage fell to 16.3% by 1960, and estimates for succeeding decades have fallen to less than 10% (Hernandez, 1993).

Reappearance of Widespread Child Poverty

A final revolution described by Hernandez (1993) pertains to the changing distribution of children across relative income levels and, as such, to a growth of child poverty, especially during the 1980s. After the Great Depression, the relative poverty rate among children dropped from 38% in 1939 to 27% in 1949 (Hernandez, 1993). During the 1950s, this rate dropped further, to 24%, and by 1969, the rate was 23% (Hernandez, 1993).

However, between 1969 and 1988, this trend of decreasing relative poverty among children reversed, and by 1988, relative poverty among children had grown by 4% (Hernandez, 1993). In other words, during the 1980s, the percentage of children living in poor families returned to the comparatively high level seen about 40 years earlier, in 1949 (Hernandez, 1993). And the percentage of children living in middle-class comfort decreased between 1969 and 1988, from 43% to 37% (Hernandez, 1993).

In summary, then, Hernandez (1993) embeds children within an historically changing matrix of variables involving family structure and function and other key institutions of society (e.g., the educational system and the economy). The import of Hernandez's scholarship for the present discussion is that at any one point in time the American family is a product of multidimensional historical changes in the contexts of human development. As such, historical variation (a) provides a basis for the diversity of the family that exists at any point in time and (b) suggests the parameters of changes that may influence the future course of the family and of human development more generally.

Moreover, other examples exist of the significance of contextual variation for human development other than those pertaining to the family. A key instance here, especially insofar as it pertains to building outreach programs that address the problems of youth developing in poor or low-income neighborhoods, involves the needs and assets of communities.

Diversity in the Characteristics of Poor Communities

Given the historical record in child development research of insensitivity to the general environment, or context, within which children develop (Bronfenbrenner, 1977, 1979; Hagen et al., 1990), it is not surprising that little attention has been paid to the variation that exists *within* any given setting. After all, if the context in general has not been of particular concern to child development researchers, then it is understandable that even less interest has been shown about the potential importance for development of either variation across or variation within contexts (Elder et al., 1993).

One instance of a lack of attention to important contextual diversity occurs in respect to poor or low-income communities (Kretzmann & McKnight, 1993; McKnight & Kretzmann, 1993). Often these neighborhoods are seen to be exclusively characterized by needs and deficits. For instance, McKnight and Kretzmann (1993) note that such settings may be often aptly characterized as being comprised of slum housing, crime gangs, drug abuse, and the other neighborhood needs depicted in the "map" presented in Figure 3.1.

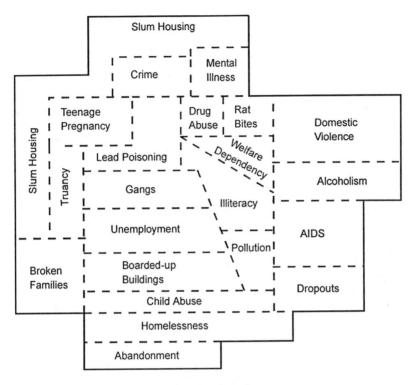

Figure 3.1. An example of a neighborhood needs map.
SOURCE: McKnight and Kretzmann (1993). Reprinted with permission.

However, although these needs are, in fact, often all present in such communities, a sole focus on such problems will result in a significant underestimation of the capacity of the community for marshaling the human, and even fiscal, resources necessary for the design and implementation of programs promoting positive features of human development. McKnight and Kretzmann (1993) note that poor neighborhoods have assets such as cultural and religious organizations, public schools, citizen associations, and the other assets depicted in the map presented in Figure 3.2. Unless attention is paid to these assets, that is, to the fact that there is diversity involving *both* needs and resources, only a deficit model of poor communities will be available to inform ideas for policies and programs pertinent to the people living in such settings. As such, both research and outreach

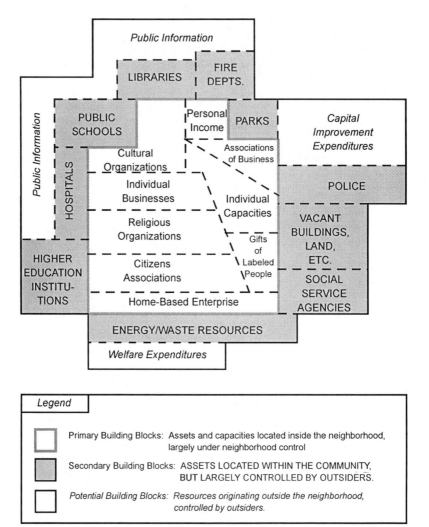

Figure 3.2. An example of a neighborhood assets map.

SOURCE: McKnight and Kretzmann (1993). Reprinted with permission.

will underestimate the human capital that exists and that may be enhanced in poor and low-income communities.

In sum, diversity of people and their settings means that one cannot assume that general rules of development either exist for, or apply in the same way to, all children and families. Moreover, one cannot assume, even if only small portions of the total variance in human behavior and development reflect variance that is unique to an individual or group, that this nonshared variance is not the most salient information we have when attempting to understand or enhance the quality of the lives for the person or group. Accordingly, a new research agenda is promoted. This agenda would focus on diversity and context while attending to individual development, contextual changes, and the mutual influences between the two.

Simply, from a developmental contextual perspective, integrated multidisciplinary and developmental research devoted to the development of programs, the study of practices, and the study of diversity and context should be moved to the fore of scholarly concern. In addition, however, scholars involved in such research would have at least two other concerns, ones deriving from the view that basic, explanatory research in human development is, in its essence, intervention research.

IMPLICATIONS FOR POLICIES AND PROGRAMS

To be complete, the integrative research promoted by a developmental contextual view of human development must be synthesized with two other foci. Research in human development that is concerned with one or even a few instances of individual and contextual diversity cannot be assumed to be useful for understanding the life course of all people. Similarly, policies and programs derived from such research or associated with it in the context of a researcher's tests of ideas pertinent to human plasticity cannot be assumed to be applicable, or equally appropriate and useful, in all contexts or for all individuals. Accordingly, developmental and individual-differences-oriented policy development and program (intervention) design and delivery would need to be integrated fully with the new research base for which I am calling (Lerner & Miller, 1993; Lerner et al., 1994).

As emphasized in developmental contextualism, the variation in settings within which people live means that studying development in a standard (for example, a controlled) environment does not provide information pertinent to the actual (ecologically valid), developing relations between individually distinct people and their specific contexts (for example, their particular families, schools, or communities). This point underscores the need to conduct research in real-world settings and highlights the ideas that (a) policies and programs constitute natural experiments, that is, planned interventions for people and institutions; and (b) the evaluation of such activities becomes a central focus in the developmental contextual research agenda I have described.

In this view, then, policy and program endeavors do *not* constitute secondary work, or derivative applications, conducted after research evidence has been compiled. Quite to the contrary, and consistent with Lanier's (1990) concept of interventionist inquiry, policy development and implementation, and program design and delivery, become integral components of this vision for research; the evaluation component of such policy and intervention work provides critical feedback about the adequacy of the conceptual frame from which this research agenda should derive (cf. Lanier, 1990). This conception of the integration of multidisciplinary research endeavors centrally aimed at diversity and context, with policies, programs, and evaluations, is illustrated in Figure 3.3.

A vision of the integration between developmental research and policies and programs was articulated more than two decades ago by Bronfenbrenner (1974). Bronfenbrenner argued that engagement with social policy not only enhances developmental research but, consistent with the developmental contextual perspective, also augments understanding of key theoretical issues pertinent to the nature of person-context relations. Bronfenbrenner (1974) noted that

> in discussions of the relation between science and social policy, the first axiom, at least among social scientists, is that social policy should be based on science. The proposition not only has logic on its side, but what is more important, it recognizes our proper and primary importance in the scheme of things. The policymakers should look to us, not only for truth, but for wisdom as well. In short, social policy needs science.
>
> My thesis in this paper is the converse proposition, that, particularly in our field, science needs social policy—needs it not to guide our organizational activities, but to provide us with two elements essential for any scientific endeavor—vitality and validity. . . . I contend that the pursuit of [social policy] questions is essential for the further development of knowledge and theory on the process of human development. Why essential? . . . [Because] issues of social policy [serve] as points of departure for the identification of

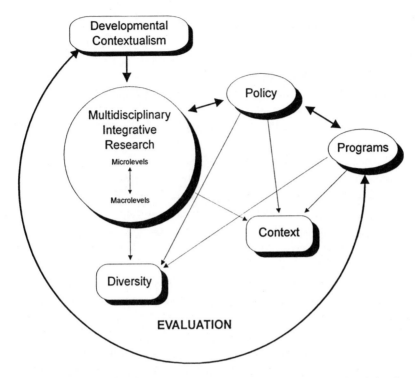

Figure 3.3. A developmental contextual model of the integration of multilevel, multidisciplinary research aimed at diversity and context, with policies, programs, and evaluations.

significant theoretical and scientific questions concerning the development of the human organism as a function of interaction with its enduring environment—both actual and potential. (pp. 1-2, 4)

To be successful, this developmental, individual differences, and contextual/ecological view of research, policy, and programs for human development requires not only collaboration across disciplines. In addition, two other types of collaboration are required. It is useful to discuss these collaborative activities in relation to themes that might organize the future activities of the individuals involved in studying and enhancing human development.

TOWARD THE CREATION OF AN INTEGRATED AGENDA

A new research and outreach agenda is brought to the fore by a developmental contextual perspective. This agenda should focus on individual diversity and contextual variation and on the mutual influences between the two. Simply, integrated multidisciplinary and developmental research and outreach devoted to the study of diversity and context must be moved to the fore of scholarly concern.

Second, this integrative research and outreach must be synthesized with two other foci: First, as just implied, this research must be integrated with policies and programs, and second, this research must involve collaborations among disciplines and between scholarly and community interests.

In regard to the first focus, I have just noted that research in human development that is concerned with one or even a few instances of individual and contextual diversity cannot be assumed to be useful for understanding the life course of all people. Similarly, policies and programs derived from research insensitive to diversity and context cannot hope to be applicable, or equally appropriate and useful, in all settings or for all individuals. Accordingly, developmental and individual-differences-oriented policy development and program design and delivery must be integrated with the new research base. Indeed, when attempts are made to explain the diversity of changing person-context relations that characterizes the human life course, then research-derived outreach becomes a means to test developmental contextual models of change processes. To be successful, these endeavors require more than collaboration across disciplines. In addition, two other types of collaboration are necessary.

First, multiprofessional collaboration is essential. Colleagues in the research, policy, and intervention communities must plan and implement their activities in a synthesized manner to successfully develop and extend this vision. All components of this collaboration must be understood as equally valuable, indeed as equally essential. The collaborative activities of colleagues in university extension and outreach; in program design and delivery; in elementary, middle (or junior high), and high schools; in policy development and analysis; and in academic research are vital to the success of this new agenda for science and outreach for children, adolescents, parents, and their contexts, for example, their extended families, their schools, their workplaces, and their communities.

Second, then, given the contextual embeddedness of these synthetic research and outreach activities, collaboration must occur with the people we are trying both to understand and to serve. Without incorporation of the perspective of the community into our work—without the community's sense of ownership, of value, and of meaning for these endeavors—research and outreach activities cannot be adequately integrated into the lives we are studying.

This view is exemplified by the work of Wilson (1987; see also Obermiller, 1991) in regard to the study of poverty among inner-city African Americans. Wilson argued that the thoughts and experiences of the poor, the people who have actually experienced poverty first-hand, were absent from the typical sociological analyses of the impact of poverty on human life. By incorporating the voice of the poor into the data he collected as part of his Chicago Urban Poverty and Family Life Project, Wilson has been able to develop a data set that more validly reflects the texture and meaning of lives lived under conditions of persistent and pervasive poverty. As such, the data set provides a basis for policy and program design that is apt to be significant for poor people; for instance, services derived from the information Wilson (1987) had obtained may be more user friendly (Forsythe, 1991) for poor people, because their voice would be a basis for the design and delivery of these services.

Thus, from a developmental contextual perspective, research that "parachutes" into the community from the heights of the academy (i.e., that is done in a community without collaboration with the members of the community) is flawed fatally in regard to its ability to understand the process of human development. This is the case because human development does not happen at the general level (Lerner, 1988, 1991); it does not occur in a manner necessarily generalizable across diverse people and contexts. Development happens in particular communities, and it involves the attempts of specific children and families to relate to the physical, personal, social, and institutional situations found in their communities. Without bringing the perspective of the community into the plan for research, then, the scholar may very likely fail to address the correct problems of human development—the ones involved in the actual lives of the people he or she is studying. And if the wrong problem is being addressed, any "answers" that are found are not likely to be relevant to the actual lives of people. Not surprising, these answers will be seen all too often (and quite appropriately) as irrelevant by the community.

In turn, however, if the community collaborates in the definition of the problems of development that they and their collaborators are facing, and if they participate in the construction of the research process, then answers that are obtained will be more likely to be the ones that they wish to know. The answers will be ones more apt to be used to build community-specific policies and programs. Moreover, community empowerment and capacity building occur by engaging in a collaborative process wherein the community places value and meaning on, and participates in, the research and outreach being conducted within its boundaries (Dryfoos, 1990, 1994; Schorr, 1988).

THE ROLE OF APPLIED DEVELOPMENTAL SCIENTISTS

Of course, such community empowerment is neither easy to facilitate nor free of problems for scientists pursuing an integrated research and outreach agenda. As noted earlier, scholars undertaking such an agenda have been termed applied developmental scientists (Fisher & Lerner, 1994; Fisher et al., 1993).

The pervasive and burgeoning problems of American individuals, families, and communities that have been discussed throughout this book have been an impetus for the development of an area of scholarship termed applied developmental science (ADS). Scholars from several disciplines (ones associated with the American Psychological Association, the Society for Research in Child Development, the Society for Research on Adolescence, the International Society for Infant Studies, the Gerontological Society of America, the National Black Child Development Institute, and the National Council on Family Relations) came to the realization that issues of child and youth development, of economic competitiveness, of environmental quality, and of health and health care were interdependent and thus required creative *and integrative* research and the design, deployment, and evaluation of innovative public policies and intervention programs. Moreover, as a consequence of the presence of the interrelated problems confronting American society, there has been over the past decade an increasing societal pressure for universities, and for the scholars within them, to design and deliver knowledge applications addressing the problems of individuals and communities across the life span.

These applications involve the ability to understand and assist the development of individuals who vary with respect to cultural and ethnic background, economic and social opportunity, physical and cognitive abilities, and conditions of living (e.g., in regard to their family, neighborhood, community, and physical settings). Infants at biological or social risk (e.g., due to being born into conditions of poverty), gifted children or those with developmental disabilities, adolescents considering health-compromising behaviors, single- and dual-worker parents, the frail elderly, and ethnic minority and impoverished families are just some of the populations requiring applications of knowledge based on the work of scholars—in fields such as psychology, sociology, nursing, human ecology/human development, social work, criminology, political science, medicine, biology, anthropology, and economics—who adopt a developmental perspective to their science.

The multiplicity of disciplines called on to apply their scientific expertise in the service of enhancing the development of individuals, families, and communities has resulted in a collaboration among the above-noted learned societies. These groups have organized the National Task Force on Applied Developmental Science to synthesize research and applications aimed at describing, explaining, and promoting optimal developmental outcomes across the life cycle of individuals, families, and communities.

To accomplish these objectives, the National Task Force has defined the nature and scope of ADS and has held a national conference (at Fordham University, in October 1991), titled "Graduate Education in the Applications of Developmental Science Across the Life Span," to inaugurate ADS as a formal program of graduate study and to specify the key components involved in graduate education in ADS (Fisher et al., 1993).

The National Task Force has indicated that the activities of ADS span a continuum of knowledge generation to knowledge application that includes, but is not limited to,

1. Research on the applicability of scientific theory to growth and development in natural, that is, ecologically valid, contexts
2. The study of developmental correlates of phenomena of social import
3. The construction and use of developmentally and contextually sensitive assessment instruments

4. The design and evaluation of developmental interventions and enhancement programs

5. The dissemination of developmental knowledge to individuals, families, communities, practitioners, and policymakers through developmental education, written materials, the mass media, expert testimony, and community collaborations

This articulation of ADS activities by the several scholarly societies involved in the National Task Force has, in a sense, involved the rearticulation of the philosophy and scholarly and outreach agenda of the land-grant university (Lerner & Miller, 1993; Miller & Lerner, 1994). That is, consistent with a developmental contextual model, applied developmental scientists seek to synthesize research and outreach to describe, explain, and enhance development in individuals and families across the life span (Fisher & Lerner, 1994). Fisher and her colleagues (Fisher et al., 1993) characterize the principles, or core substantive features, of ADS in terms of the following five conceptual components:

1. Temporality of change. There is a temporal component to individuals, families, institutions, and community experiences. Some components remain stable over time; other components may change. The temporality of change has important implications for research design, service provision, and program evaluation.

2. Sensitivity to individual differences and within-person change. Interventions must take into account individual differences, which means the diversity of racial, ethnic, social class, and gender groups.

3. Centrality of context in terms of individual families and of family development. Context exists at all levels—biological, physical/ecological, sociocultural, political, economic, and so on—and invites systemic approaches to research and program design and implementation.

4. Emphasis on (descriptively) normative developmental processes and on primary prevention and optimization rather than on remediation.

5. Respect for the bidirectional relationship between knowledge generation and knowledge application.

Moreover, given the developmental contextual model involved in ADS, scholars in this field assume that

there is an interactive relationship between science and application. Accordingly, the work of those who generate empirically based knowledge

about development and those who provide professional services or construct policies affecting individuals and families is seen as reciprocal in that
research and theory guide intervention strategies and the evaluation of interventions and policies provides the bases for reformulating theory and
future research. . . . As a result, applied developmental [scientists] not only
disseminate information about development to parents, professionals, and
policy makers working to enhance the development of others, they also integrate the perspectives and experiences of these members of the community into the reformulation of theory and the design of research and
interventions. (Fisher & Lerner, 1994, p. 7)

Thus, for applied development scientists, community empowerment is
not only seen as an important outcome of their scholarship. It is, at the
same time, a key component of the collaborative process through which
they conduct their scholarship. Accordingly, for applied developmental
scientists, community empowerment means that people will have an increased capacity to advocate for, *and* collaboratively contribute to the development of, the outreach activities they value and the resources they
require to sustain these efforts.

However, the advocacy component of community-collaborative outreach raises some ethical issues for applied developmental scientists: How
can applied developmental scientists retain their stance as objective program designers and/or evaluators if they are part of a clearly value-based
advocacy effort? In other words, how do applied developmental scientists
respect the inherent advocacy component of community-collaborative
outreach programs without sacrificing the unique and critical role they
play within this collaboration, that is, as scholars whose commitment to
science assures that the appropriateness and effectiveness of services are
evaluated objectively?

Moreover, given findings from life-span development (Baltes, 1987;
Hetherington, Lerner, & Perlmutter, 1988) that imply that appropriate
evaluation may require long-term, longitudinal study, and given the limited funds available for outreach efforts much less for the evaluation of
them, the applied developmental scientist must also determine the conditions under which it is ethical to (a) conduct short-term evaluation research and/or (b) maintain that the evidence from such evaluations
provides justification for a given advocacy effort.

I do not here have answers to these ethical issues, nor do I even want to
here suggest a range of options (but see Fisher & Tryon, 1990, for a discussion

of such a range). Rather, the point of these examples of ethical issues that will arise in the sorts of community collaborations likely to be involved in an integrated approach to research and outreach is to indicate the complexity of the intellectual tasks facing tomorrow's applied developmental scientist, that is, the scholar pursuing a developmental contextual agenda.

Yet I believe that I have illustrated the importance and rewards of undertaking such difficult and challenging work: A developmental contextual perspective promotes collaboration *with* communities (and not just research or outreach *in* communities). By linking the academy's scholarship with an empowered community, developmental contextualism provides theoretically innovative, methodologically rigorous (von Eye, 1990a, 1990b, 1990c), but complex and arduous, means to build relevance into the study of human development.

This relevance is underscored by the results of evaluations of programs intended to prevent the sets of behavioral problems and risks, and the sequelae (or the rotten outcomes) (Schorr, 1988) of persistent and pervasive poverty, that we have seen today beset increasing numbers of America's youth. The analyses of scholars such as Dryfoos (1990, 1994, in press), Schorr (1988, 1992), and Hamburg (1992) indicate that programs, consistent with several of the concepts involved in the integrated research and outreach agenda forwarded by developmental contextualism, promote the prevention of many of the behavioral risks and rotten outcomes confronting our nation's children and adolescents. That is, concepts pertaining to the emphasis in developmental contextualism on diversity, context, the relational character of human development, and multiprofessional and community-wide collaborations appear integral both to effective prevention programs *and* to building successful life spans through the actions involved in these programs.

In other words, the analyses of Dryfoos, Schorr, and Hamburg illustrate the integrative model displayed in Figure 3.3, that is, the model indicating that—within developmental contextualism—there is a synthesis of basic and applied research. The evaluation of actions that are designed to enhance the course of development may elucidate both the nature of useful interventions and the bases of positive youth development. It is useful to review, then, the features of successful prevention programs and to discuss their consistency with developmental contextual ideas.

4

Designing Successful Prevention Programs

What are the hopes and aspirations we have for our children? Health, happiness, and a successful and productive life are the ones that often come to mind. In actuality, these desires are not very different from those that many people who study children and adolescents find associated with positive youth development. To illustrate, the Carnegie Council on Adolescent Development (1989, pp. 15-17) has envisioned five qualities that characterize a youth who has developed well through the middle school years. Specifically, such a youth would be

1. *An intellectually reflective person,* analyzing problems and issues, developing new solutions, having good self-expression and listening skills, and being competent in understanding the perspectives of multiple cultures

2. *A person en route to a lifetime of meaningful work,* seeing work both as a means of economic survival and a source of self-definition; feeling that race, gender, and ethnicity do not limit his or her career options; understanding the importance of high school graduation and postsecondary training; and—to be able to adjust to a world of changing economic and employment circumstances—having the ability and motivation to continue learning across the life span

3. *A good citizen,* contributing responsibly to the events and institutions (e.g., the schools) of his or her community; understanding the values of our nation and acting to promote these values across all levels of our society; and feeling responsible for enhancing the health of the community at local, state, national, and international levels

4. *A caring and ethical individual,* thinking and acting ethically; understanding the difference between good and bad; accepting responsibility for his or her actions; showing honesty, integrity, tolerance, and appreciation of diversity; and developing and maintaining close relationships with family and friends

5. *A healthy person,* showing physical and mental fitness, having a positive self-image, maintaining self-understanding, and possessing appropriate coping skills

How can American society foster these attributes of positive youth development? Clearly, given the multifaceted individual, interpersonal, and institutional character of these attributes, neither one person nor a single institution (e.g., the family) can be charged with sole responsibility in promoting the positive development of youth. Thus all segments of the community—the entire "village" (Miller, 1993), including local, state, national, and even international portions of the village—must collaborate in the raising of our nation's youth. Indeed, given the historically revolutionary changes that have occurred in the American family over the course of this century (Hernandez, 1993), children's and adolescents' families are less able than perhaps ever before to act alone in fostering positive youth development.

Accordingly, arguably more so than at any other time in our history, America's families need support from other sectors of their communities to both promote the positive development of youth and, as well, to take steps to prevent the actualization of the risks and problems facing today's children and adolescents. In other words, community-based youth programs are a vital part of what must be a "village-wide" response to foster positive life development among America's youth. Moreover, given the pervasiveness of the problems of today's youth (Dryfoos, 1990; Hamburg, 1992; Schorr, 1988), there is no community wherein such community-based programs are not needed.

The Carnegie Corporation of New York (1992) reports that today, in America, there are about 17,000 organizations that provide community-based youth programs. As described in the Carnegie Corporation (1992) report, these programs are associated with a range of organizations. On the one hand, there are large, national organizations that are rich in staff and, often as well, are *relatively* secure in financial resources; examples are the Girl Scouts of the USA, the YMCA, and the 4-H programs that are part of each state's Cooperative Extension Service. On the other hand, there are local (grassroots) organizations, entities that may have few staff and limited resources. Within this range exist organizations such as adult service and/or civic clubs (e.g., Kiwanis and Rotary), sports organizations (e.g., Little League), and groups associated with local and state governments (e.g., municipal departments of parks and recreation or teen health programs of state departments of public health).

Community-based programs can make several potential contributions to positive youth development. As noted by the Carnegie Corporation (1992) report (see also Villarruel & Lerner, 1994), these contributions include the following:

Providing opportunities for youth to engage in positive social relationships with peers and adults. Mentoring and coaching relationships, and both the formal and the informal activities within which they occur, help youth develop social skills and provide them with prosocial alternatives to delinquent and gang behavior (cf. Mincy, 1994).

Teaching youth important life skills. Programs, by facilitating and providing models for skills such as goal setting and decision making, group cooperation and teamwork, problem solving, and communication, enable youth to develop abilities that will be important across their lives (Carnegie Corporation of New York, 1992; Villarruel & Lerner, 1994).

Offering youth opportunities to make contributions to their communities. Programs that involve youth in service to the community enable them to develop leadership skills, engage in cooperative learning and decision making, and develop a refined sense of community and, through giving of themselves to their community, help to instill an understanding of the importance of philanthropy (Villarruel & Lerner, 1994).

Providing youth with a sense of being part of a positive group experience. Humans are biological, psychological, and social organisms (Erikson, 1959; Tobach & Schneirla, 1968). Social relationships are an essential part of human life; if groups providing positive youth development are not available to young people, the lessons of history (e.g., see Erikson's, 1950, discussion of "Hitler's Youth") and of research (Lerner & Spanier, 1980; Mincy, 1994) teach us that youngsters will gravitate to delinquent groups to find the social relationships they need. Accordingly, community-based youth programs offer both formal and informal means through which children and adolescents may develop a sense of belonging to groups committed to enhancing the individual and collective lives of the community.

Facilitating the sense of self-competence among youth. A positive sense of self is a key component of healthy development across the life span (Harter, 1988). Children's and adolescents' sense of self involves perceptions of self-competence in the areas of academic ability, social relationships, physical/athletic ability, and the adequacy of conduct (Harter, 1982, 1983). By the provision of opportunities to be involved in positive social relationships with peers and adults, by teaching youth important life skills, by offering youth opportunities to make contributions to their communities, and by providing youth with a sense of being part of a positive group, community-based programs provide youth with a set of experiences that increases the probability that they will develop both a multifaceted sense of self-competence and the actual behavioral competencies they will need to increase their chances of having happy, successful, and productive lives.

The actualization of these potential contributions of community-based youth programs is of vital importance to the welfare of our nation's youth and to the health of our nation. Many youth have a good deal of discretionary time available to them. The Carnegie Corporation (1992) estimates that only 60% of adolescents' waking hours involve essential activities such as school, homework, meals, paid employment, or chores around the home. In turn, then, for 40% of their time, adolescents can choose to do what they want and, as the Carnegie Report (1992) notes, much of this discretionary time is "unstructured, unsupervised, and unproductive for the young person" (p. 10). Indeed, many youth spend much of their discretionary time by themselves (Carnegie Corporation of New York, 1992).

Thus community-based youth programs can offer youth a constructive alternative to using their discretionary time in unproductive ways. Moreover, by building the bases of positive youth development, these programs can act as an important means to prevent the actualization of the risks confronting America's youth.

However, many youth programs are not fulfilling their potential. As noted by the Carnegie Corporation (1992), many community-based programs are fragmented: Their component services are uncoordinated; their focal activities are aimed at only one of the interrelated set of problems confronting youth (e.g., either substance problems, sexuality problems, school problems, *or* crime problems) (Dryfoos, 1990) and not on the combined impact of the co-occurrence of these problems; and the content of the programs may not have sufficiently rich or motivating activities. In addition, many local and even state-related programs are seriously underfunded, have low staff morale, and do not provide adequate training for adult leaders (Carnegie Corporation of New York, 1992).

Furthermore, as the Carnegie Corporation (1992) report notes, there is one other quite disturbing characteristic of many current youth-serving programs: They focus their services on youth from more advantaged families. In other words, poor urban or rural youth are not the prime audiences of these programs, and even when these youth are participants in these programs, the short duration of the program (e.g., 1 or 2 hours a week is not atypical) does not afford enough support to ensure the benefits needed from the program.

All is not bleak, however, in regard to youth programs. Although youth programs do not fulfill their potential for many of the reasons noted above, there are numerous instances of such programs in fact working well—that is, of programs promoting positive youth development and preventing the actualization of the risks confronting children and adolescents. In many respects, the characteristics of these successful programs are a mirror image of the characteristics of unsuccessful programs. However, even successful programs face important problems—if not of program structure or function per se, then of long-term program viability, of program sustainability. Thus, even for successful youth programs, there is both good news and bad news. It is important to discuss both of these attributes of successful programs.

THE GOOD NEWS AND THE
BAD NEWS OF SUCCESSFUL YOUTH PROGRAMS

Dryfoos (1990), Schorr (1988), and Hamburg (1992) have reviewed the results of evaluations of youth programs aimed at preventing the profound risks and problems besetting contemporary American youth in general and poor and low-income youth in particular: drug and alcohol use and abuse; unsafe sex, teenage pregnancy, and teenage parenting;

school failure, underachievement, and dropout; unemployability; prolonged welfare dependency; feelings of despair and hopelessness; and delinquency and, often violent, crime. The overall import of the results of the evaluations of the several dozen programs reviewed by Dryfoos (1990), Schorr (1988), and Hamburg (1992) is quite encouraging: There are numerous programs that have been shown to effectively prevent the risks and problem behaviors associated with contemporary youth development. Similarly, Rick Little (1993), Secretary General of the International Youth Foundation (IYF), notes that there are over 1,300 programs worldwide that have been identified as successful in preventing problems of youth development. Moreover, the successful prevention programs noted by Dryfoos, Schorr, Hamburg, and Little have several characteristics in common, and, as well, these characteristics appear to be associated with a clear set of principles. Thus there is a knowledge base that can be used for the design of potentially successful programs.

However, despite this good news provided by the work of Schorr (1988), Dryfoos (1990), and Hamburg (1992), there is also some less welcome information derived from their scholarship. Despite the identification of hundreds of effective programs, and despite the fact that many of these programs had stood the test of evaluation in the demonstration of their effectiveness, most programs were not sustained. For example, about 50% of the programs identified by Schorr (1988) as having been evaluated to be effective prevention interventions were no longer in existence only *1 year* after Schorr visited them. And after 2 years, the percentage remaining in existence grew even smaller. Moreover, Little (1993) notes that the issue of sustainability is often overlooked in most youth programs and by program developers. He believes that to adequately address the issue of sustainability, youth organizations and programs must begin to discuss the issue of how a program will endure "moving" funding targets, reduced budgets, and program and personnel costs (Little, 1993).

In addition, Little (1993) notes that program sustainability is related to the issue of organizational capacity. He believes that too many programs are based on one person's ideas, and he observes that although "idea people" start programs, they often need others to organize, manage, and sustain the program. From the perspective of the IYF, successful programs have an organizational infrastructure that supports the various types of activities that are involved in creating and sustaining a youth-serving organization. Specifically, these organizations have more than one person who develops programs and programmatic ideas (Little, 1993). More important, successful organizations have staff specifically devoting their time and energy to finances, management, strategic planning, and fund raising (Little, 1993).

Thus, even though there is knowledge about what works, and successful programs can be identified, policies, funding "streams," organizational capacities, and incentives are often not in place to sustain such endeavors. The absence of sustainability may also be due in part to the fact that academic researchers who demonstrate that a program works have no incentives to show that it can continue to work. Neither publications nor additional funding are likely to ensue from showing that a successful program maintains its success. In turn, both private foundations and governmental agencies are more apt to fund new demonstration projects than they are to support either replications in other communities or continuations of efforts in the same community.

Given such circumstances, a demonstration that a program works is unlikely to be coupled with personnel or resources from outside a given community to sustain the program after the demonstration period is completed—a fact made evident by the disappearance of the effective programs identified by Schorr (1988). Accordingly, when the demonstration program parachutes out of the community, just as it was likely to have parachuted into the community when it began, the community will likely feel less hopeful and less empowered than it did before the program was begun. That is, the hopes for improvement in the lives of the children and families of the community may have been enhanced by the success of the program. But because these disappearing programs did not leave the community with the capacity to sustain the success after the period of the demonstration project was completed, these raised hopes may ultimately be dashed. Rather than a successful program, what might be left are feelings of loss and disappointment, or even of exploitation and anger.

To avoid such unfortunate residues of the disappearance of successful programs, it would seem that programs must include as a key design component actions that enhance the capacity of community members to themselves sustain the program. Although it is of course the case that funding philosophy and policies (of private foundations and government agencies) must change to allow resources to be obtained by an empowered community seeking to sustain an effective program, it is also the case that successful programs often do include community capacity building as a prime objective. I will return to a discussion of policy issues below; here, however, it is useful to discuss the several features of successful programs that have been identified by Dryfoos (1990) and Schorr (1988).

FEATURES OF SUCCESSFUL PROGRAMS

Developmental contextualism stresses that diversity and context should be the focus of both research and outreach efforts. Consistent with these foci, Dryfoos (1990) notes that a primary feature of successful programs is intensive and individualized attention to the participants in the program. Thus an emphasis on the diversity of the people in the program is key. This diversity includes race, ethnicity, culture, physical ability status, and—as Hamburg (1992) emphasizes—the developmental level of the people in the program. Similarly, Little (1993), in formulating the 17 criteria used by the IYF to identify successful youth programs, also stresses that the activities of good programs are developmentally appropriate.

Moreover, Hamburg (1992) notes that in successful programs any incentives used for program participation must be relevant to the lives of the youth. This is another key instance of diversity, then: Knowledge of the individual's specific motivations, interests, aspirations, and needs will be critical if incentives are to be effective. Little (1993) makes comparable points. The IYF, which focuses on successful prevention/early intervention programs aimed at enhancing development of children and adolescents between the ages of 5 and 20, believes that effective programs are ones that meet the identified needs of the participating children and adolescents. Moreover, rather than focusing on either remediation or treatment, successful prevention programs seek to meet youth needs by promoting positive development in regard to one or more of the following four attributes, all characteristics that Little (1993) believes are key developmental requirements of young people:

1. *Competence.* Effective programs help youth develop practical skills to sustain and improve the quality of their lives (e.g., by building literacy; employability; interpersonal, vocational, and academic skills; sensitivity to environmental issues; and the ability to contribute to their cultures).
2. *Connection.* Successful programs promote the development of caring human relationships (e.g., through mentoring, peer tutoring, peer counseling, intergenerational programs, leadership opportunities, or community services).

3. *Character.* Successful programs promote values that give meaning and direction to the lives of children and adolescents. Examples of such values are individual responsibility, honesty, community service, concern for equity, committed relationships, responsible decision making, and courage (Little, 1993).

4. *Confidence.* Effective programs provide experiences that lead to hope and self-esteem. For instance, such programs provide youth with early and sustained success experiences and the opportunity to set and meet goals.

In essence, then, Little (1993) believes that if youth-serving programs promote these four characteristics the developmental needs of children and adolescents will be successfully met, positive youth development will be enhanced, and the actualization of risk will be prevented. In a similar vein, Schorr (1988) stresses that successful prevention programs design their services to be responsive to the individual needs of the people most at risk. In addition, she notes that to create programming that is sensitive to these significant problems of the individual requires establishing a non-bureaucratic program culture, one that is user friendly and that continues to evolve to be increasingly responsive to the individual needs of the people the program is attempting to serve.

Hamburg (1992) also stresses the importance of user friendliness. He indicates that successful programs have social rules and behavioral expectations that are clear to youth and respected by them; when these characteristics are present, programs provide youth with a predictable environment. Moreover, stressing the need for the individual to be an active agent in the program, a key point emphasized within developmental contextualism, Hamburg (1992) notes that successful programs promote active youth participation and provide the opportunity to learn new skills.

Moreover, Schorr (1988) emphasizes that such focus on the individual allows a program to have, at its core, a preventive orientation. That is, through a focus on the individual and his or her distinctive needs, a program may be able to strengthen and empower the person for long-term, healthy development (Little, 1993). Similarly, Dryfoos (1990) emphasizes that successful programs incorporate early identification and intervention: Such program components serve to enhance individual capacities, and they have a better chance of avoiding the actualization of risk and thus the need to have to rely on ameliorative interventions to reduce the already crystallized presence of problematic behaviors.

Furthermore, Dryfoos (1990), Schorr (1988), and Hamburg (1992) emphasize that the focus on the individual must occur within a program structure that integrates key features of the context within which the individual is embedded. For instance, Hamburg (1992) notes that successful programs promote relationships among multiple supports in the youth's context. Little (1993) agrees with this view. Among the 17 criteria the IYF uses to identify successful programs is the idea that an effective program meaningfully involves parents and/or extended family and/or other significant adults. Similarly, Dryfoos (1990) indicates that successful prevention programs for adolescents involve the four social institutions essential to development during this period: family, peer group, workplace, and school. In other words, to be effective, prevention programs for adolescents must engage:

A youth's family. Parents must be involved because of the continued salience of the family for healthy development in the adolescent period (Allison & Lerner, 1993); that is, there are several features of family life that foster healthy development—not only in adolescence but, as well, during childhood. Hamburg (1992) has identified several of these features of the family. Among these are an intact, cohesive, and dependable nuclear family; a parent-child relationship marked by love and nurturance; an experienced parent who enjoys raising his or her child, who can cope with the stresses of childrearing, and who enjoys teaching his or her child; social support provided by the extended family; and the provision to the child of predictable adult behavior and of a family context that inculcates in the child a vision of a positive, adult future.

A youth's peers. Peers must participate in the program because of the increased salience of the peer group during this period of life (Lerner, 1988) and because peers have credibility with other adolescents (Hamburg, 1992). Thus, even with many of the most difficult problems of adolescence (e.g., drug use, unprotected sex), well-trained peers can help other youth build skills to resist engagement in risk behaviors and, in turn, to pursue healthier behavioral options (Hamburg, 1992). Moreover, when peer involvement takes the form of a tutor-tutee relationship, there are often personal, social, and academic benefits for both youth (Hamburg, 1992).

The world of work. The workplace must be engaged because (a) it has become an increasing presence in contemporary adolescents' lives (e.g., about 60% of all adolescents enrolled full time in high school work part time) (Steinberg, 1983) and (b) unless intervention programs during adolescence are linked to a successful transition to adult life, which, centrally, involves engagement in productive and socially useful employment, any positive developments produced by the programs will be wasted. In this regard, Hamburg (1992) notes that preparation for work is a key component of a multifaceted set of skills needed by adolescents for them to become successful citizens of the modern world:

> Democratic societies are now challenged as never before to give all our children, regardless of social backgrounds, a good opportunity to participate in the modern technical world, especially in preparation for modern employment opportunities; to achieve at least a decent minimum of literacy in science and technology as a part of everyone's education heritage; to make lifelong learning a reality so that people can adjust their knowledge and skills to sociotechnical change; and to foster a scientific attitude useful both in problem solving throughout society and understanding the major issues on which an informed citizenry must decide. (p. 332)

The role of schools. In regard to the school as a key social institution involved in successful prevention programs, Dryfoos (1990) first indicates that such programs involve community-wide, multiagency collaborative—and integrated—approaches, that is, approaches wherein agency or program "turf" is ceded for the benefit of providing a comprehensive and integrated focus on the totality of the individual and his or her context and not on artificially segmented portions of his or her individual and/or social functioning. Hamburg (1992) places similar stress on the importance of integrated and comprehensive services. Moreover, Schorr (1988) also indicates that successful prevention programs involve integration—of children within the family and, as well, families within their communities. Moreover, Schorr also notes that such programs must be comprehensive; in addition, however, because of the need to attend to the individual and to what may be his or her changing needs over the course of participation in the program, programs need to be intensive (i.e., long term), flexible, and responsive.

Thus Dryfoos (1990), Hamburg (1992), and Schorr (1988) indicate that programs should not promote and, by implication, policies should not mandate (or perhaps even allow) the separate focus on mental health, public health, social service, and educational issues. Rather, programs (and policies) should promote an integrated, case management approach to services. Similarly, one of the criteria used by the IYF to identify successful programs is that the features or components of a program must be appropriate in multiple contexts; they must promote cross-setting continuity (Little, 1993). Thus, to Little (1993), such a program would be coordinated, as appropriate, with the services of other child and adolescent programs. Indeed, programs that are the most successful frequently are those that partner with other youth-serving institutions to expand the number of youth who might benefit from these (integrated) programs (Little, 1993).

That is, Little (1993) observes that the vast majority of youth-serving programs reach only very small numbers of youth. However, programs that grow in their scale (i.e., in the number of youth served) do so through such integrative partnering. Moreover, to increase in scale in this manner, Little (1993) believes that information about the program and about its impact must be disseminated from the outset of a program. This dissemination should be part of program planning and should be conceived and conducted with an intent to build scale-enhancing partnerships. As such, dissemination must be predicated on the question, "How do *we* do it?" (i.e., enhance the scale and success of our program), and not on the question, "What's in it for me?" (Little, 1993).

In essence, then, such integrated approaches will emphasize the specific needs of the individuals and contexts served by the program and will avoid the personal and familial fragmentation that may accompany being embedded in a system wherein one is compelled to "be served" by several disconnected agencies and programs. In addition, such integration will save money; it will avoid the creation of "million dollar families," that is, families who are served by several disconnected programs. Finally, an appropriately and successfully integrative program will have several other features. As articulated in the criteria used by the IYF to identify effective youth-serving programs, these features include a cost-effective means of achieving program goals (due, at least in part, to the money saved through integration), which, in turn, is related to the presence of organizational resources and capacities (both formal and informal) to (a) enact program activities and (b) serve a greater (and, potentially, a significant) number of youth (through integrative partnering) (Little, 1993).

Where may the integrated and comprehensive services discussed by Schorr (1988) and Dryfoos (1990) be located? Dryfoos (1990) finds that successful prevention programs having these features are often located in schools. In contemporary American society, the school is the institution wherein the largest number of our nation's children and adolescents can be reached at one time, both in terms of number of hours per day that youth are in school and in terms of number of years in which they remain in school.

However, Dryfoos (1990) finds that when school-based programs are successful they are administered by nonschool agencies. That is, the school gives up some of its turf to other community agencies and programs who, in turn, integrate their delivery of services within schools. When this collaboration occurs between the school and the youth- and family-serving agencies and programs within the community in which the school is embedded, an integrated and comprehensive community-wide system is established. Dryfoos (1994, in press) terms this entity a full-service school.

I will discuss in Chapter 5 some of the details of full-service schools. Here, however, it is important to note that in addition to being embedded within community-wide, multiagency integrated structures, such as full-service schools, successful programs have several other distinctive features.

The Importance of Training

Dryfoos (1990), Schorr (1988), and Little (1993) stress that training in the features of the program and in social skills are among the most important of these features. Often, the personnel delivering a program are not experienced in the substance of the program or are not familiar with the principles of human development that pertain to the children, adolescents, and families participating in the program. Thus Little (1993) stresses that successful programs include initial training plus follow-up training and support for project staff and other participants, as needed. Moreover, program personnel may not possess the particular social skills requisite for interacting effectively with the specific children, adolescents, and families participating in a program. The need for social skills training will be increased if it is the case that program personnel are not from the same socioeconomic, cultural, racial, or ethnic backgrounds as are the program participants.

Hence successful programs include arrangements for training in the sub-stance of the program, for education about the developmental and cultural characteristics of the program participants, and for building *culturally competent* social skills (Dryfoos, 1990; Schorr, 1988). Indeed, Little (1993) notes that, in successful programs, the content, strategy, and leadership of the program are appropriate to the culture of the community. Accordingly, with provisions for the inculcation of culturally appropriate knowledge and skills, programs thereby support the establishment of trusting and meaningful re-lationships among program personnel and participants (Schorr, 1988).

Finally, to be successful in continuing a program over time, personnel must have, or be trained to possess, the ability to develop a feasible plan to become self-sustaining in financial support, in facilities and materials, in leadership, and in continuing to address identified needs (Little, 1993). Moreover, according to the IYF, programs that have staff trained in this way standardly include as part of the functioning of the organization planning, monitoring, evaluation, and feedback (Little, 1993). Furthermore, successful programs are those that, to the greatest extent possible, include the youth par-ticipants not only in these organizational activities but, as well, in the im-plementation of, and dissemination about, the program (Little, 1993).

Building a Caring Community

Finally, Dryfoos (1990), Schorr (1988), and Little (1993) stress that ef-fective programs, although they may be primarily located in schools, need to also be situated in the community more pervasively. That is, children and adolescents are not always in schools: They spend time on the streets of their neighborhoods, in other youth-serving institutions (e.g., 4-H clubs), hanging out at malls or at friends' homes, or just being by them-selves (Carnegie Corporation of New York, 1992). These contexts must not become cracks through which our youth fall. Communities must pro-vide continuity of programming efforts that extend to all portions of neighborhoods, and community members must assure that all youth in need of a program have access to it (Hamburg, 1992). For instance, the IYF notes that successful programs are built on a community approach that includes (a) involving multiple sectors of the community, (b) being re-sponsive to locally identified needs, and (c) a process for building thor-ough community/neighborhood participation (Little, 1993). In short, the community must ensure that, no matter where a child or adolescent goes in the community, he or she is supported and protected.

Hamburg (1992) provides an excellent example of the importance of such a community-wide commitment to children through a recounting of his memories about the neighborhood of his childhood years:

> Many of those memories have to do with "Second Street," the house my grandparents bought in Evansville, Indiana, the city where my grandfather settled soon after his arrival [in the United States]. This house became the family headquarters. My grandparents raised their seven children there, and in time, the house became a kind of community center—not just for their seven children and their many grandchildren, of whom I was the first, but also the regular gathering place for other relatives, neighbors, and friends.
>
> The door at Second Street was always open. When I was a child, my parents and I would drop in several times a week to visit. We never knew which relatives and friends we would find, but we could always count on lively conversation, warmth, and support. Everyone shared ideas and information freely, alerted others to new opportunities, and offered help to whoever needed it. (pp. 3-4)

Thus programs that are focused in schools must also be embedded thoroughly in the complete fabric of the community. We must adopt the ethos—once prevalent in America's communities but, now, more difficult to find—that all children in the community are our children. We must take the responsibility, and give each other the right, to prevent youth risk behaviors whenever and wherever we see them. If we turn our backs on our youth, if we do not work to extend the meaning and intent of effective, school-based programs to the entire community and build a seamless social support net for our children and adolescents, then not only "their" children, but our children, and indeed all of us, will suffer in numerous and historically unprecedented ways.

The importance, then, of Schorr's (1988) idea, that effective programs see children both as part of families and as part of the community, seems clear. Similarly, the truth of the now often-cited African proverb, that it takes an entire village to raise a child, has never appeared more certain. It will take the efforts of every citizen in a community to protect adequately their children and adolescents, and, in turn, to increase to the level of absolute certainty the chance of every member of their younger generations to maximize his or her potential for healthy and productive development.

CONCLUSIONS

Successful prevention programs integrate features of the developing individual with those of his or her specific community context. In addition, such programs inculcate in program personnel knowledge of the substance of the program and competence in understanding the development and culture of the diverse children, adolescents, and families participating in the program.

These characteristics of successful prevention programs are consistent with the core ideas of diversity and context stressed in developmental contextualism. In addition, from the reviews of features of successful prevention programs presented by Dryfoos (1990) and Schorr (1988), several principles of successful programming may be derived. These principles are also consonant with the ideas associated with developmental contextualism. It is useful to turn to a discussion of these principles involved in successful prevention programs.

5

Key Principles of
Successful Prevention Programs

The problems of contemporary American children and adolescents were not produced by a single event or derived from a single cause. Neither poor parenting; poverty; inappropriate media influences; inadequate health care; problems of local, state, and federal economies; a failed educational system; racism; territoriality among social service and other youth- and family-serving agencies; nor inadequate state and federal policies alone produced the problems faced by America's children. However, all these phenomena are a part of the developmental system within which America's children are embedded (Ford & Lerner, 1992), and it is this system that is implicated in the production of the problems of our nation's youth.

Given, then, that development in the context of this system provides the bases of these problems, this same system has to be engaged in any comprehensive solution to these problems. As such, and as Dryfoos (1990) points out, *there is no one solution to a problem of childhood or adolescence.* The developmental system may be—and, for comprehensive and integrated solutions, must be—engaged at any of the levels of organization represented in Figure 2.4. Thus, for any particular problem of youth behavior and development, for example, youth violence, solutions may be sought by, for instance, entering the system at the level of the individual, his or her family, the community, or the societal/cultural context (e.g., through working to affect social policies).

A second reason why recognition of the potential for multiple solutions to a problem is important is that *high-risk behaviors are interrelated.* As noted by Dryfoos (1990), 10% of all 10- to 17-year-olds in America engage in behaviors associated with all four major categories of high-risk behaviors (i.e., drug and alcohol use and abuse, unsafe sex, school failure, and delinquency and crime). Similarly, Schorr (1988) notes that poverty is associated with several rotten behavioral outcomes, for example, school failure and dropout, unemployability, prolonged welfare dependency, and delinquency and crime.

The interrelation as well as systemic bases of high-risk behaviors means, then, that no one type of program is likely to be of sufficient scope to adequately address all the interconnected facets of a problem. Instead, as Dryfoos (1990) notes, *a package of services is needed within each community.* However, because of the systemic interconnections of the problems this package is to address, program comprehensiveness, in and of itself, will not be adequate. Rather, *an integration of services is required.*

Moreover, because of the systemic nature of the problems of children and adolescents, the integrated services that are provided to address these problems should be directed to this system and not solely at the individuals within it. In other words, the relations—among individuals, institutions, and levels of the context—provide both the bases of the problems of children and adolescents and potential sources of change in these problems. As such, *interventions should be aimed at changing the developmental system, within which people are embedded, rather than at changing individuals* (Dryfoos, 1990).

Moreover, because of the systemic nature of youth problems and of their potential solutions, *the timing of interventions is critical* (Dryfoos, 1990; Lerner, 1984). That is, across life, the developmental system not only becomes more organized but this organization also involves, in a sense, overorganization; in other words, redundant, as well as alternative, portions of the system function to support developmental functioning (Hebb, 1949; Schneirla, 1957). For example, problem behaviors in adolescence may involve emotional shortcomings on the part of a youth (e.g., low self-esteem) *and* poor child-rearing skills on the part of his or her parents *and* negative appraisals about, and loss of hope for, the youth by school personnel *and* a peer group that promotes norm-breaking or even illegal behavior; each part of this system may reinforce, support, or maintain, the adolescent's problem behaviors. Accordingly, problems of behavior and development, once embedded in this redundantly organized system, are more difficult to alter than is the case if the same problems were embedded in the system at an earlier portion of its development (Clarke & Clarke, 1976; Ford & Lerner, 1992; Lerner, 1984).

It is the case that the developmental system remains open to intervention across the life span of individuals; that is, there is relative plasticity in human behavior and development across life (Lerner, 1984). Nevertheless, the above-noted developmental changes in the organization of a system over the course of life mean that to effect a given change in behavior or development, interventions occurring later in life require greater expenditures of effort and require involvement of greater portions of the system than is the case in earlier portions of the life span (Baltes & Baltes, 1980; Clarke & Clarke, 1976; Ford & Lerner, 1992; Lerner, 1984).

Accordingly, preventive interventions are more economical—in terms of time, scope, and other resources—than are ameliorative interventions. An excellent illustration of this point is provided by Hamburg (1992). Young, pregnant adolescents have a higher probability than do postadolescent females of giving birth to a high-risk baby, that is, a low-birth-weight and/or premature baby. Hamburg (1992) notes that the total cost of good prenatal care for a pregnant adolescent would be much less than $1,000. However, the intensive care that would be needed to keep a low-birth-weight or premature baby alive would be at least $1,000 a day for many weeks or months. Often, the initial hospital cost of such care is $400,000 (Hamburg, 1992). Thus preventive prenatal care for pregnant adolescents would not only save a lot of money but, as well, would eliminate the sequelae of emotional, behavioral, social, and physical problems—for both mother and infant—associated with the birth of a high-risk baby. Yet most pregnant adolescents, especially those under 15 years of age, receive either no prenatal care or inadequate care (Hamburg, 1992). Moreover, about 50% of pregnant adolescent African Americans do not receive prenatal care or they receive care only in the last 3 months of pregnancy (Hamburg, 1992). Moreover, poor, inner-city, and isolated rural youth are among those most likely to have no or inadequate prenatal care (Hamburg, 1992).

Thus, as illustrated by the information Hamburg (1992) presents about the economic and human benefits of preventing high-risk births through prenatal care, preventive interventions—although insufficiently used—

seem most efficacious in the promotion of healthy youth and family development. That is, although the relative plasticity of human behavior and development across the life span means that there is always some probability the intervention can be successful, the nature of the developmental system indicates that prevention has the best likelihood of effecting desired changes.

Of course, a system that remains open to changes for the better also remains open to changes for the worse. Thus the interventive means through which human behavior and development change is *not* akin to inoculation to disease. Accordingly, one-shot interventions into human behavior and development are unlikely to effect enduring changes.

Instead, interventions must be designed to be longitudinal in scope (Lerner & Ryff, 1978) or, as both Dryfoos (1990) and Hamburg (1992) note, *continuity of programming must be maintained across development.* Programs, conceived of as life-span convoys of social support (Kahn & Antonucci, 1980), should be implemented to protect and enhance the positive effects of preventive interventions.

Clearly, such continuity of effort is expensive. However, a commitment to life-span programming must be coupled with a commitment to *discontinue programs that have proven to be ineffective* (Dryfoos, 1990). Accountability, the requirement to deliver a high-quality program, is a necessary feature of professionally responsible, ethical, and humane programs (cf. Hamburg, 1992). Moreover, if only those programs that have been shown to be effective are continued, then resources devoted to poor programs may be saved. Of course, making such decisions requires that appropriate evaluation information exists.

However, as noted by Little (1993), one of the most difficult barriers to overcome for most youth-serving programs is evaluation. He observes that, all too often, evaluation is not central, is underfunded, or is not a part of program development. Little indicates that for the programs that IYF has identified as providing models of best practice, evaluation is a key feature of the program, and, in addition, evaluation involves the use of variable data. That is, the evaluations go beyond the use of mechanistic input-output data associated with traditional models of evaluation. Rather, these evaluations include the perspectives of the stakeholders of a program, and this information is used to guide, enhance, and inform the evaluation process (Little, 1993).

In essence, then, Little (1993) stresses that successful youth-serving programs not only standardly include evaluation as a core part of their activities but, as well, approach evaluation by involving stakeholders in the organization and implementation of the evaluation. At the same time, however, Little (1993) alerts us to the fact that this participatory and potentially community-stakeholder-empowering approach to evaluation is not a traditional means through which the effectiveness of youth-serving programs is determined. It is important to focus on key distinctions, highlighted by Little (1993), in how to evaluate the success of youth-serving programs.

BUILDING THE CAPACITY OF YOUTH AND
FAMILIES THROUGH COLLABORATIVE EVALUATION METHODS

As implied by Little (1993), the nature of evaluation is, indeed, a complex and controversial issue (Cronbach and Associates, 1980; Jacobs, 1988; Lerner, Ostrom, & Freel, in press; Ostrom, Lerner, & Freel, 1994). Building on trends in evaluation methodology begun in the 1960s (Weiss & Greene, 1992), many approaches to evaluation rest on the belief that "phenomena exist in pure, protean forms, uncontaminated by environment" (Jacobs, 1988, pp. 40-41). Such positivistic views of evaluation lead to a decontextualized assessment of programs; in other words, such views result in an evaluation that involves an experimental design, that is, a comparison of the outcome behaviors of program participants with those of a control group (Weiss & Greene, 1992); evaluators using such a method typically seek to assess only cause-effect relationships between the presence of a program and variation in specified outcomes. That is, the program is seen as a discrete and holistic event—as one level of a dichotomous independent variable, or treatment, where the other level is "no program."

Such approaches to evaluation are typically used to inform "an audience of legislators, program funders, and other remote decision makers" (Weiss & Greene, 1992, p. 133), but these approaches typically do not consider the variation within a program, for example, the processes through which the content of a specific program is formed. In addition, such experimental approaches do not usually consider the manifestation of a specific program in a particular community, the meaning of and values about a given program in a specific community, and thus the possibility that a given program may be formed and may function in quite different ways in different communities (Weiss & Greene, 1992).

Other, more recent approaches to evaluation use methods that enable such possibilities to be entertained. These more diverse approaches find an impetus in the need for programs—and the evaluation of the quality of life promoted through them—to speak to the concerns and values of multiple groups of stakeholders, including program participants themselves. Moreover, variation in evaluation methodology derives from an evolution of understanding about what is important to learn about a program. In addition to wanting to know the outcomes of a program, both stakeholders and evaluators have come to want to know how better programs can be formed. For instance, key issues here are the identification of the components of programs that work well, are not effective, or could be improved; the means to address such issues often involve qualitative as well as quantitative methods, and, as such, case studies, questionnaires, interviews, surveys, and ethnographic observations are often employed (Weiss & Greene, 1992).

Furthermore, to address the issues pertinent to forming better programs, the specific perspectives of different stakeholders about a program's strengths and liabilities and about how to improve a program have been recognized to be important to incorporate into evaluations. Again, the combination of the above-noted qualitative and quantitative methods has been recognized as useful in incorporating the voices of diverse stakeholders into the formative evaluation process. Inclusion of the perspectives—the values, meaning systems, and experiences—of all stakeholders into the evaluation process adds an important feature to the development of programs. Such inclusion constitutes an important means to empower youth, families, and other community stakeholders to become central participants in the enactment of programs promoting valued goals. As a consequence, such inclusion can promote sustained community change (Weiss & Greene, 1992).

Building a Participatory-Normative Approach to Evaluation

The arguments for such an approach to evaluation have been championed by Weiss and her colleagues (e.g., MacDonald, 1994; Miller, 1993; Weiss, 1987a, 1987b; Weiss & Greene, 1992; Weiss & Hite, 1986; Weiss &

Jacobs, 1988), collaborating through the Harvard Family Research Project. For instance, Weiss and Greene (1992) note that a value-based, or normative, approach to evaluation, one that as well engages the community and, especially, the youth and family program participants in the design, implementation, and analysis of the evaluation, empowers the community and enhances the efficacy of the program. In other words, a participatory and normative approach to evaluation

- Builds on the values and meaning system of the youth, families, and other stakeholder groups in the community
- Engages this community coalition as active participants (partners) in the evaluation
- Enhances the capacity of the community partners to themselves identify, organize, and use their assets (McKnight & Kretzmann, 1993) to conduct planned actions (i.e., programs) to attain goals they value

Thus the participatory-normative approach to evaluation envisioned by Weiss and Greene (1992) serves to counteract the often irrelevant, uninformative, and disempowering nature of many evaluations of youth- and family-serving programs; it serves this end by enfranchising community stakeholders as full partners in the decisions for programs and their evaluations and the judgments about the programs. By building a program from the inside, that is, by enabling diverse stakeholders—and especially the most disenfranchised and least empowered ones—to voice their understanding of the problems of their community, and of the way in which a program may or may not help address this problem, evaluation is incorporated, at the start of a program, as a core feature of the program's intervention (Weiss & Greene, 1992). Both the program and its evaluation are constructed through an initial qualitative understanding of the values, meaning system, and desired goals for the program and, more broadly, for the community. Simply, a participatory-normative approach to evaluation is a value-added component to an intervention in that, through the collaborative conduct of the evaluation, the capacity of community stakeholders to better direct their own future development is enhanced.

To illustrate, Weiss and Greene (1992) note that

> an emphasis on participant and sometimes on community empowerment has been a central tenet and operational goal of the family support movement. . . . Like the Maternal Infant Health Outreach Worker Project (MIHOW),

family support programs with an empowerment orientation encourage individual social and personal growth and economic progress by building on
participant strengths (rather than remediating deficits) and by creating
partnerships to work *with* parents to convey information and to support
parental competence and growth. These programs assume parents have the
ability to help themselves and each other, and are structured to assist them
in doing so. The way in which program services are delivered and the empowering and supportive nature of participant-staff relationships are as important as what services are delivered. Such programs also aim to engender
more collective action and change by anchoring project activities to salient
community concerns.

In markedly parallel fashion, the MIHOW program's evaluation emphasized an empowering orientation by giving voice to program participants'
concerns and by facilitating their growth and development through involving them as collaborators in the evaluation process. Such empowerment-
oriented evaluations sometimes go further in their aim to promote more
structural social change by also involving established decision makers in the
evaluation process and by centering the evaluation within the local community context. Empowerment programs and empowerment evaluations, that
is, share a common value base and a common set of ends or goals for
individual and collective change. We believe that considerable mutual benefits can accrue—and that the shared values and ends can be importantly
advanced—by a joining together of empowerment programs and normative,
participatory evaluation approaches, so that program and evaluation activities work in tandem, rather than comprise distinct, even conflictual arenas
of thought and conversation. (pp. 131-132)[1]

The Development-in-Context Evaluation (DICE) Model

Promoting positive individual and social development and change
through the incorporation of participatory evaluation into program design and implementation is precisely what is considered within a developmental contextual view of evaluation (Lerner et al., in press; Ostrom et al.,
1994). Indeed, from a developmental contextual perspective, which emphasizes a community-collaborative approach to the integration of research and outreach, *program- and community-specific evaluation is a
requisite for all effective programming* (Dryfoos, 1990) and for an understanding of the basic processes of human development (Lerner, 1991).

Accordingly, such evaluations will seek to understand how a successful
program may be designed, implemented, assessed, and sustained in a spe-

cific community. To attain such knowledge, a development-in-context evaluation (DICE) model may be pursued (Lerner et al., in press; Ostrom et al., 1994). The DICE model is an instance of the sort of community-evaluator collaborative, participatory-normative approach to evaluation forwarded by Weiss and Greene (1992).

Moreover, the DICE model builds on the basic tenets of the philosophy of pragmatism in general (Dixon & Lerner, 1992), and on Charles Sanders Peirce's (1905) pragmatic maxim specifically. Peirce's conception of pragmatism focuses on the results or consequences that will occur if one accepts and acts on any idea, theory, model, policy, or innovation. Several ideas flow from this seemingly straightforward maxim. The key ones guiding the DICE model are the following:

Think holistically or contextually. There is nothing gained by making a theoretical or practical distinction between the program/innovation and the context within which it occurs.

Include as many voices or stakeholders as possible (cf. Weiss & Greene, 1992). To the extent that some perspectives and voices are excluded from relevant and decisive conversations, then the consequences related to those points of view are silenced. As a corollary, evaluators must be competent in understanding the cultural diversity of the various stakeholders involved in the program (Dryfoos, 1990) and the different points in the life span (i.e., the different developmental levels) of the youth, families, and other community stakeholders (e.g., aged community members with no young children) with whom they work.

The focus is on the actions involved in forming effective programs, not on "getting things right." As Jacobs (1988) notes, evaluation is best viewed as the systematic collection and analysis of program-related data that can be used to understand how a program is functioning and/or what consequences the program has for the participants (pp. 49-50).

Reality is complex and socially constructed (i.e., based on the perspectives present within the community context). Not only are there a huge number of details that may be assimilated about any program, there are also situations in which cause and effect are subtle and where their effects over time are not obvious. To construct a sufficiently rich mosaic, it is necessary to include as many of the different perspectives, or frames of reference, present in the community as possible.

Evaluation is a core and essential component of every program and should be built into the program's day-to-day functioning (see Weiss & Greene, 1992). There are numerous purposes for an evaluation (Jacobs, 1988). Primary among these are that evaluations should be formative and should have a focus on use. As Cronbach and Associates (1980) note: "The better and more widely the workings of social programs are understood, the more rapidly policy will evolve and the more the programs will contribute to a better quality of life" (pp. 2-3). As a corollary, evaluations must not detract from the operation of the program and should, in fact, seek to form the basis of more functioning of the program (Weiss & Greene, 1992).

Using Asset Mapping to Launch Program and Evaluation Activities

To implement these pragmatic ideas, evaluations—and the programs of which they are an inherent, initial part—must build from the inside out (McKnight & Kretzmann, 1993); that is, the initiation of programs and evaluations must involve looking for solutions or assets within the community. As discussed earlier, Kretzmann and McKnight (1993) observe that there are two paths that communities can take when seeking solutions to pressing problems. The first, and more traditional, approach begins by focusing on a community's needs, deficiencies, and problems, and the second begins with a clear commitment to discovering a community's capacities and assets.

The first, traditional, approach provides images of needy, problematic, and deficient communities populated by needy, problematic, and deficient people and leads to programs that teach people about their problems and the value of "service" provided *for* them as the answer to their problems. The people begin to view themselves as people with special needs that can only be met by outsiders. Young people can begin to see themselves "as fundamentally deficient, victims incapable of taking charge of their lives or their community's future" (Kretzmann & McKnight, 1993, p. 4). Focusing only on needs or deficits also leads to other problems as well: fragmentation, funding going to service providers and not to the community, undermining of the local leadership, deepening of the cycle of dependence, creating a maintenance and survival strategy, and thwarting community development.

The second, alternative, path is capacity focused and leads to the development of programs based on the capacities, skills, and assets of children, parents, and other community stakeholders. From this perspective, solutions to problems must come from the inside out. A thorough map of community assets would begin with an inventory of the capacities of the children, parents, and other residents of the community. This would be augmented with an inventory of community organizations; these formal and informal organizations are the means through which citizens assemble to solve problems or share common interests. Finally, the asset map includes the more formal institutions that are located in the community. Simply, individuals, community organizations, and local institutions constitute the asset base for every community.

This second path to community problem solving is based on three straightforward and interrelated characteristics. First, the process of building programs should be asset based. The program should start with what is in the community—the capacities of the residents and of the programs, agencies, and other institutions based in the area—not with what is absent. Second, the program should be focused on building an agenda for program development based on the perspectives, values, and problem-solving capacities of local residents, local associations, and local institutions. Consistent with the participatory-normative approach to evaluation forwarded by Weiss and Greene (1992), the internal, community-based focus stresses "the primacy of local definition, investment, creativity, hope, and control" (Kretzmann and McKnight, 1993, p. 9). Third, this second path is predicated on the importance of building strong and positive relationships among local residents, local associations, and local institutions—on creating a collaborative, caring community.

FEATURES OF DEVELOPMENT-IN-CONTEXT EVALUATIONS

Taken together, the ideas of pragmatism and of asset mapping provide an approach to evaluating how programs may enhance the development of youth and families within their community context that has four components: evaluation design, data collection, data analysis, and using evaluation findings to promote sustained community change.

Evaluation Design

The hallmark of evaluation design is that it pays attention to stakeholders' perspectives (for example, about programs and possible solutions), to assets, and to the diverse array of sound evaluation methods available to address the issues present in a community. Thus this phase of the evaluation constitutes a key instance of the importance of a colearning model and of the potential fruitfulness of a community-university collaboration.

University faculty may have knowledge about how to identify, organize, and help deploy community-based assets; they may also have knowledge about how to enable diverse stakeholders to give voice to their values and perspectives about community issues; finally, faculty may have knowledge about the uses and limitations of different types of existing features of evaluation methodology and about how to develop new evaluation tools (e.g., assessment or screening instruments). However, university faculty must learn from community members about what development in their particular community context means. Faculty must learn from the community the people, agencies, programs, and institutions that should be included in an asset map. They must network with community members to learn (a) who are the people whose voices must be included as part of the program and its evaluation and thus (b) the issues that the community wants to have addressed and that are seen as most salient. Finally, faculty must learn what specific evaluation tools are necessary and appropriate to deploy or to develop in the community.

The goal of a development-in-context evaluation is, then, to work collaboratively with the relevant stakeholders to identify and describe the problem, articulate program goals, and identify the types of questions that the community wants to have answered. Within the boundaries set by the stakeholder-evaluator collaboration, the strongest and most appropriate evaluation design, for the community and for the issues it sets as of the highest priority, is formulated.

Data Collection

Given the array of issues and methods that may need to be used in any given community, the possible approaches taken to data collection must be similarly multifaceted. As noted above, this range of information-gathering strategies encompasses a broad array of both qualitative and quantitative techniques (Weiss & Greene, 1992). However, the goal of any technique that is used is to provide the information that youth, families, and other community stakeholders will need to address the questions of interest, monitor (assess) the ongoing effectiveness of the program, improve the functioning of the program, and assess the extent to which program goals are being realized.

Data Analysis

By using both qualitative and quantitative methods, development-in-context evaluations are able to engage in "triangulation"; such evaluations are able to identify whether similar information is obtained by different methods. If such convergence occurs, then it is more certain that the information is valid (and not just the artifactual product of a specific type of method).

Different methodologies are sensitive to different aspects of program functioning. Development-in-context evaluations are based on attention to the natural ecology of the community (Bronfenbrenner, 1979) and take a developmental systems view (Ford & Lerner, 1992) of the interconnections among the levels of organization that exist within this ecology—including the relationships among youth, families, and the social and institutional networks within which they are embedded.

Accordingly, just as multiple methods must be used to ascertain the validity of information and to appraise the multiple levels of the developmental system, data analysis does not involve a single computational technique or an analysis of information derived from only one point in time (e.g., as might be the case if only program outcomes were of interest). Instead, data analysis is focused on the actual operations and impacts of the program as they occur longitudinally, that is, over the course of the development of the program and of the youth and families participating in it.

A key goal here is to obtain interpretations of the day-to-day realities of the people, programs, and contexts involved in the program. Again, then, colearning is essential here: The participants themselves are the experts of the meaning of development in their community context; they are the source of the important interpretations of the data. It is their values and the meaning they attach to the ongoing information developed about the program that will be a critical source of both community empowerment and, as a result, of the capacity of the community to sustain the program (Weiss & Greene, 1992).

Using Evaluation Findings to
Promote Sustained Community Change

Through collaborating with community stakeholders in the interpretation of the data obtained about the program, evaluators assist stakeholders in determining whether the findings are appropriate for the needs of the community. If so, stakeholders will be in a position to make judgments about the features of the program that should be maintained, revised, or eliminated. If not, stakeholders will be better able to clarify for the evaluator the sort of information they need to make such judgments. In either case, however, the capacity of the stakeholders to make better informed decisions about their community will be enhanced.

Such an increased capacity constitutes a new asset for the community; it is a value-added contribution of the sort of participatory-normative evaluation approach forwarded by Weiss and Greene (1992) and found with the DICE model. Moreover, when program-pertinent information is developed through the stakeholder-evaluator collaboration—as it will almost necessarily eventually be, given the increased capacity of the community and of the colearning involved in the university-community partnership—the capacity of the community to enhance the development of programs within its boundaries will be, in effect, also enhanced. This second instance of capacity building constitutes another value-added contribution of the approach to evaluation embodied in the DICE model.

Finally, the program itself, initiated, maintained, and improved over time by an increasingly empowered community, is a third new asset introduced by the collaborative evaluation process. Accordingly, the capacity of youth, families, and other community stakeholders to enact and to sustain desired programs will likely be furthered significantly as a consequence of (a) the community's enhanced abilities in program design, implementation, and evaluation; (b) community members' increased knowledge of themselves, gained through the data that they themselves helped collect and analyze (e.g., through assessments such as asset mapping and through the ongoing data collected as part of the process of forming a better program); and (c) the community's increased experiences with successful decision making, that is, with what is a constant part of the process of participatory evaluation procedures such as those involved in the DICE model.

To summarize, then, the DICE model represents an instance of the community-collaborative, participatory-normative approach to evaluation—*and* to program design, program development, and community empowerment—promoted by Weiss and her associates (e.g., Jacobs, 1988; Miller, 1993; Weiss, 1987a, 1987b; Weiss & Greene, 1992; Weiss & Jacobs, 1988). As such, evaluators following the DICE model:

- Work with community members to identify the problems or issues to which the program will be directed
- Engage the members of the community in (a) the planning of the evaluation; (b) decisions about the nature of any preliminary, developmental, and outcome information sought about the program; (c) the collection of relevant data; and (d) the interpretation of the information derived from the evaluation
- Collaborate with the community in the use of the information derived from the evaluation, for example, in the execution of any "midcourse" corrections deemed necessary to enhance program effectiveness and/or in the identification of any changes that have resulted in the nature of the problem that led to the initiation of the program

Moreover, evaluations conducted within the framework of the DICE model build from a qualitative understanding of the community and of the goals for the program envisioned by community members; as well, such evaluations collaborate with the community throughout the entire process of gaining the knowledge that the evaluation seeks to obtain. This is why such evaluations involve at their core *colearning* between the evaluators and the community. In addition, the community-collaborative approach of such evaluations builds the capacity of the community to sustain the program after the evaluation is completed; indeed, the community is empowered to incorporate continued evaluations into its future plans about the program.

Finally, such evaluations are predicated on attention to the diversity that exists within a specific community, to the specific goals, values, and meaning systems that are present in the community and that shape the program. Recognition of the importance of such diversity appears critical in the design of effective prevention programs. As noted by Dryfoos (1990), *programs that pay attention to cultural and lifestyle diversity as well as to individual diversity are more likely to succeed.*

DEVELOPMENTAL CONTEXTUALISM
AND PROGRAM DESIGN AND EVALUATION

The concepts of developmental contextualism and the features and principles of successful prevention programs, especially when they involve a participatory, development-in-context approach to evaluation, appear to be highly consonant. Accordingly, the application of developmental contextual ideas and the principles of successful programs should assist in the design, implementation, evaluation, and sustainability of programs effectively addressing the problems of children and adolescents. Although, by necessity, specific features of such programs will vary in relation to the particular target problem(s) being addressed and the particular community within which the program exists, it is clear from the above discussion that these programs will share some general features. They will involve integrated, community-wide, multiagency (or institutional) collaborations that link youth, families, and the larger community together in a sustained effort.

As noted above, the work of Dryfoos (1990, 1994, in press) suggests that full-service schools may represent a concept in programming that exemplifies the features of a successful prevention program. Accordingly, to illustrate the specific characteristics of the type of child and youth program brought to the fore by a developmental contextual perspective, it is useful to discuss the concept of full-service schools.

THE POTENTIAL ROLE OF
PROGRAMS INVOLVING COMMUNITY-WIDE,
INTEGRATIVE MULTIAGENCY COLLABORATIONS:
THE SAMPLE CASE OF FULL-SERVICE SCHOOLS

America's schools are intended to promote the intellectual and social development of students. Schools are also intended to be contexts for the inculcation of cultural values and for the development of a citizenry competent to pursue healthy individual and family lives and to contribute productively to our nation. As summarized by the Carnegie Council on Adolescent Development (1989), the goals of schools are the development of intellectually reflective, healthy, caring, and ethical people, good citizens on the path to lifetimes of meaningful work.

However, because of changes in the nature of the American family across this century (Hernandez, 1993) and due to the growth of child and youth poverty, violent crime among adolescents, and the incidence of other risk behaviors (Dryfoos, 1990; Huston, 1992; Schorr, 1988), schools are increasingly charged with providing services that were, in prior historical periods, the aegis of other social institutions (Dryfoos, 1994). For instance, Alvarez (in press) notes that "until recently and for centuries, young generations were integrated into society via their families. During this century, school experiences became the *conditio sine qua non* to participate in the benefits of social life in most places in the world" (p. 1).

Failures of America's Schools

All too often, schools are not fulfilling these functions: School programs and school structures frequently fail to provide a goodness of fit with the complex health, social, and cognitive needs of youth (Ames & Ames, 1989; Dryfoos, 1994; Eccles & Midgley, 1989). This failure is derived in part from at least three interrelated problems (Dryfoos, 1994; Lerner, 1994).

First, schools are not adequately addressing the problems presented by the large proportions of America's youth engaging in one, and often several, high-risk behaviors. Accordingly, other community-based organizations may have to help address these problems. Indeed, Alvarez (in press) notes that "today, thousands of youth programs are complementing, and in some cases supplementing, the role of families and schools" (p. 1).

Second, the increasing prevalence of youth poverty is challenging the resources of schools and is diminishing the relevance and utility of current portfolios of school-based programs. As Dryfoos (in press) notes, "Schools cannot educate children who are too 'stressed-out' to concentrate. Schools were never set up in the first place to be support agencies. Teachers are not trained as social workers, and cannot possibly attend to their jobs if they must spend all their time trying to remediate problems" (p. 7).

Last and perhaps superordinately, failure is occurring because of the absence of a thorough integration of the school into the community, an integration involving the services of other youth-serving institutions, parents, and youth themselves. The superordinate nature of this third problem is captured by Dryfoos (in press), in her observation that educational experts have excellent ideas about how to improve the educational outcomes of disadvantaged children, with extensive research and demonstration models that work in low-income communities (Comer, 1989; Slavin, Karweit, & Wasik, 1994; Wehlage, Rutter, Smith, Lesko, & Fernandez, 1989). Consensus is building among educators about the importance of bringing support services into schools that will strengthen their efforts at restructuring (Usdan, 1994). Organizations such as the National Association of State Boards of Education, the National Association of School Boards, and the Council of Chief State School Officers have been in the vanguard of task forces and commissions that call for comprehensive school-based service programs. (pp. 7-8)[2]

Problems of America's Children, Families, and Communities

As emphasized throughout this book, there are numerous indications of the severity and breadth of the problems besetting our nation's youth, families, and communities; similarly, there is considerable evidence for the need to innovatively restructure schools in a manner that involves the inclusion of comprehensive, integrative services. An illustration of these problems is, as noted earlier, the fact that of the approximately 40 million children and adolescents enrolled in America's 82,000 public elementary and secondary schools about 25% of them (10 million of America's children) are at risk for school failure, for example, for failure or dropout (Dryfoos, 1994). Moreover, I have noted above that risk of school failure is interrelated with three other types of risk behaviors in adolescence: unsafe sex, teenage pregnancy, and teenage parenting; drug and alcohol use and abuse; and delinquency and (often violent) crime (Dryfoos, 1990). Furthermore, and as also noted above, child and youth poverty exacerbates the risk behaviors of adolescents: Poverty is associated with early school failure as well as with unemployability, violent crime, and feelings of hopelessness and despair (McLoyd & Wilson, 1992; Schorr, 1988).

The Potential Role of Full-Service Schools

As Dryfoos (1990, 1994, in press) suggests, there appears to be an effective strategy for America's schools to follow to address these issues: The enhancement of the role of schools in child and youth development rests on the creation of full-service schools. The state of Florida, in 1991 legislation to support comprehensive school-based programs, has defined a full-service school as one that

> integrates education, medical, social and/or human services that are beneficial to meeting the needs of children and youth and their families on school grounds or in locations which are easily accessible. Full Service Schools provide the types of prevention, treatment, and support services children and families need to succeed . . . services that are high quality and comprehensive and are built on interagency partnerships . . . among state and local and public and private entities . . . [including] education, health care, transportation, job training, child care, housing, employment, and social services. (quoted in Dryfoos, 1994, p. 142)

Such schools involve, then, in a fully integrated manner: (a) community-wide, multiagency collaborations, (b) involving a full range of social services (e.g., health centers, vocational guidance and career development programs, and counseling services), which are (c) embedded within schools but are administered by the collaborating nonschool agencies; and use (d) citizen input and volunteerism.

These components of the full-service school concept are congruent with Dryfoos's (in press) vision for these schools. In her view, the full-service school

> integrates the best of school reform with all other services that children, youth, and their families need, most of which can be located in a school building. This concept expands the Florida definition and encompasses an educational mandate that places responsibility on the school system to reorganize and innovate. The charge to community agencies is to bring into the school: health, mental health, employment services, child care, parent education, case management, recreation, cultural events, welfare, community policing, and whatever else may fit into the picture. The result is a new kind of "seamless" institution, a community school with a joint governance structure that allows maximum responsiveness to community needs, and accessibility and continuity for those most in need of services. (pp. 7-8)

In the broadest vision of full service schools, the goals of the advancement of quality education and the development of support services coexist. Restructured schools pay attention to individual differences, give staff a wide range of choices in teaching methods, organize curricula that [are] stimulating and relevant [and] get rid of tracking. The support side pays attention to all the other primary health, mental health, and social needs of the people in that particular school community. (pp. 12-13)

As explained by Dryfoos (in press), there is a great need for such innovative institutions:

Disadvantaged young people, living in run-down resource-poor communities, cannot overcome the odds without substantial assistance. Some lack family nurturing and require individual attention from surrogate parents. Many go to schools in which they are expected to fail. Both the health system and the educational system are called upon to respond to these social deficiencies. Thus the rationale for creating new kinds of institutional arrangements crosses several domains: health, education, and social services integration. (p. 4)

Moreover, Dryfoos (in press) goes on to note that

the full service schools that are being created appear to be a rational solution to a whole array of delivery problems. Needed services are co-located in one place, a center that welcomes its clientele, promises them confidential and caring services, and demonstrates a high level of concern about what happens to them. In today's beleaguered communities, this is a profound departure from the fragmented non-systems that people are supposed to rely on to help them get through their troubled lives. Even in middle-class communities, young people experience stressful circumstances and appreciate access to caring adults on the school premises.

I believe that the concept of full service schools fits well with what we know about today's young people, a portion of whom are growing up in threatening social environments with many crucial shortages. These youngsters lack parental support, go to endangered schools, live in troubled communities, and face many barriers to achievement. The concept of full service schools embraces partial solutions to many of these problems, simultaneously addressing the need for individual support, comprehensive services, parent involvement, and community improvement, in the context of school restructuring. The concept encompasses the discourse on service integration, pushing toward the combination of health, mental health, and family services, along with recreation and culture in one site, the school, open from early in the morning till late at night, weekends and summers. (pp. 37-38)

Components of Full-Service Schools

Given the comprehensive and integrative character of full-service schools, it is clear that such institutions engage children, adolescents, and their families across the life span. Emphasizing a preventive and capacity-building orientation to addressing the co-occurrence of child and youth problems, such schools provide integrated services from birth, or even prenatally, through the point that the person is launched successfully on a path involving a productive and healthy adult life. Dryfoos (1994, in press) finds that, to accomplish these ends, full-service schools typically incorporate several components of service (as distinguished from components pertinent to educational restructuring). These service components include the following:

A *planning process.* This process begins with an assessment of the capacities and needs of the community, one aimed at ensuring that the structure and function of the full-service school use the resources and meet the specific needs of the children and families of the community (cf. Kretzmann & McKnight, 1993). Here it is critical that the school and community agencies overcome turf issues and create a vision of a new type of joint institution. Thus this planning process must yield "an efficient design, utilizing the contributions of each party to building strong and durable full service schools" (Dryfoos, in press, p. 42).

A *service design process.* This process integrates new services with those health, social, and counseling services already present in the school. Thus, rather than replace existing programs, services are designed in the supplementary manner noted by Alvarez (in press).

A *collaborative governance structure.* This governance structure often takes the form of an advisory board, one that involves personnel from the school and from service agencies and, as well, parents, community leaders, and children and adolescents. This governance structure is based on an agreement among all collaborators to "pursue a shared vision and have common goals, expect to share resources, participate in joint decision-making, and use their personal and institutional power to change systems" (Dryfoos, in press, pp. 26-27).

A system to use space for primary health care and/or other services. If primary health care is provided, then an area in or near the school building is used. As noted by Dryfoos (1994, in press), this space should be used for examination rooms, a laboratory, confidential counseling rooms, and an office for referrals and files. When primary health care is not provided in or near the school, school space should nevertheless be dedicated for individual and group counseling, parent education, and case management and referrals. Furthermore, space should be allocated for career information, play, clothing and food distribution, and food preparation. In addition to providing the space for these functions, the school provides maintenance and security. Moreover, classrooms, gyms, and computer facilities remain open for use by the community, and the doors of the school remain open before and after school, on weekends, and during the summer (Dryfoos, 1994, in press).

Opportunities for building leadership. The building principal is instrumental in implementing the programs of the full-service school and in maintaining the programs' effective operation. In addition, a program director is responsible for the conduct of the services provided in the school and functions collaboratively with the governance structure.

CONCLUSIONS

Full-service schools are a promising community-collaborative vehicle for implementation of the principles of effective prevention programming. However, as Dryfoos (1994, in press) points out, the program- and community-specific evaluations necessary to adequately document the potential contributions of full-service schools have yet to be conducted. The conduct of such evaluations may be an important contribution that developmental contextual-oriented researchers can make in community collaborations in which they may participate.

In addition, the DICE model of evaluation, discussed above, suggests that such evaluations should be integrated with community-specific dissemination of information about full-service schools and with community-based education about how to implement the features of such schools. As such, there is a significant contribution that colleagues from extension can make in the community collaborations involved in such evaluations.

Indeed, I believe that, in general, partnerships between the research and extension communities are critical if the developmental contextual vision of integrated research and outreach is to succeed in producing effective programs for America's children and adolescents. Moreover, research and extension partnerships will be the vital base on which universities will be able to build effective means to respond to the problems facing America's children.

NOTES

1. Quotes from "An Empowerment Partnership for Family Support and Education Programs and Evaluations," by H. B. Weiss and J. C. Greene, 1992, *Family Science Review, 5,* pp. 131-148, are reprinted with permission from *Family Science Review.*

2. Quotes from "Full Service Schools: Revolution or Fad?" by J. G. Dryfoos, in press, *Journal of Research on Adolescence,* are copyrighted by Lawrence Erlbaum Associates, Inc. Reprinted with permission.

6

Meeting the Challenges
Facing America's Universities by
Integrating Research and Outreach

How may a university contribute to usefully addressing the problems of contemporary human life, including the issues confronting the youth and families of America's diverse communities? Clearly, paradigms of the past have been insufficient, at least as gauged by the burgeoning problems of America's children, adolescents, and families (Huston, 1992; Lerner & Fisher, 1994; Lerner, Terry, McKinney, & Abrams, 1994; McKinney et al., 1994).

It is unfortunate that much of the scholarship related to children, families, and their communities that flows from university faculty does not engage the communities involved in the scholarship. This lack of integration with the needs and world views of the community will make the findings of such scholarship difficult to translate into policies and programs of meaning and value to the community. Because such scholarship will appear distant from what the community believes is important, actions based on such scholarship will not be "owned" by the community. Moreover, when the community does not collaborate in the formulation of scholarship, any community capacity building that may accrue from such partnership is not likely to be produced (Dryfoos, 1990).

100

Developmental contextualism, however, offers a conception of research that is integrated with community needs, of scholarship that derives from a collaboration between the university and the people involved in the scholarship, scholarship that is therefore linked to community-based actions and capacity building. Indeed, research associated with developmental contextualism can be conceived of as the type of scholarship that was intended to be associated with the American land-grant university (Lerner & Miller, 1993; Miller & Lerner, 1994). Although, in recent decades, the research typically engaged in at these universities has not been consistent with the original land-grant vision (Boyer, 1990, 1994; McKinney et al., 1994; Miller & Lerner, 1994), there is a growing commitment across our nation to revitalize this traditional mission (Enarson, 1989). At least in part, the reinvigoration of this community-collaborative integration of research and service (or outreach) has been promoted by the paradigm of scholarship promoted by faculty pursuing developmental systems perspectives such as developmental contextualism (Lerner et al., 1994); these faculty have typically been associated with land-grant institutions' colleges of home economics (or their derivatives, such as colleges of human ecology or human development) (Lerner et al., 1994; Miller & Lerner, 1994). It is useful to discuss the model of scholarship promoted by the home economics tradition.

THE AMERICAN LAND-GRANT
UNIVERSITY AND THE VISION OF HOME ECONOMICS

The contemporary mission of the American land-grant university is typically stated to be teaching, research, and service (with service often used interchangeably with the terms *extension* or *outreach*). The three components of this mission and the order in which I have presented them have an important basis in the history of our nation (Enarson, 1989). A brief history of land-grant universities will show the prominent role that the field of home economics has had in fostering a vision of integrated research and outreach.

As explained by the National Association of State Universities and Land-Grant Colleges (1989), the American land-grant university system was created through the first land-grant university act, the Morrill Act, which was signed into federal law by President Abraham Lincoln on July 2, 1862. This act provided 17.4 million acres of land to the states so that each might have at least one college whose purpose was "to promote the liberal and practical education of the industrial classes in the several pursuits and professions of life." According to Bonnen (1993), the land-grant idea is democratic in a social sense and elitist in an intellectual sense. It is committed to first-class science and scholarship applied to the practical problems of society. This combination of both excellent scholarship and application to the needs of society is what represents the core of the land-grant idea.

A second Morrill Act was signed into law by President Benjamin Harrison on August 30, 1890, so that the states could provide a "just and equitable division of the fund to be received under this act between one college for White students and one institution for colored students." The enactment of this law was an impetus for the creation of 17 historically Black land-grant colleges in Southern and border states (National Association of State Universities and Land-Grant Colleges, 1989).

The Hatch Act was approved by Congress on March 2, 1887; it mandated the creation of agricultural experiment stations "to aid in acquiring and diffusing among the people of the United States useful and practical information on subjects connected with agriculture and to promote scientific investigation and experiment respecting the principles and applications of agricultural science."

The Smith-Lever Act was signed into law by President Woodrow Wilson in 1914; this law was intended to allow land-grant institutions to extend instruction beyond the boundaries of campuses. The purpose of this extension was to "aid in the diffusing among the people of the United States useful and practical information on subjects relating to agriculture and home economics, and to encourage the applications of the same." The act further specified that the cooperative extension work of land-grant institutions "shall consist of the giving of instruction and practical demonstrations in agriculture and home economics to persons not attending or resident in said colleges in the several communities, and imparting to such persons information on said subjects through field demonstrations, publications, and otherwise."

One way of representing the import of the federal acts that created the combined teaching, research, and outreach mission of the land-grant system is to depict such an institution as the university *for* the people of the state: That is, the land-grant university's functions of knowledge generation (research), knowledge transmission (teaching), and knowledge utilization (outreach) exist to improve the lives of the people of its state as they live in their communities. This land-grant mission was refined through the vision of ecologically valid and useful scholarship articulated in the field of home economics.

In 1892, Ellen Swallow Richards, the first woman faculty member in any science program in the United States (at Massachusetts Institute of Technology), proposed a science of human ecology focused on the home and the family, one labeled by her as *home oekology* (Bubolz & Sontag, 1993). Since that time, the vision of the land-grant university, as the university for the people of its state, was operationalized within the field of home economics/human ecology as a university for the children, families, and communities of its state. Moreover, the human ecology vision of the tripartite, land-grant mission was that research, teaching, and outreach should be viewed as integrated, or synthetic, activities. Teaching about the ecologically valid settings within which children and families live their lives (that is, within their homes and within their communities) or research conducted within these settings is predicated on an understanding of the needs, values, and interests of the specific people and particular community the land-grant institution is trying to serve. Accordingly, when knowledge generation or transmission occurs in a context that the community values, and that sees practical significance of these facets of knowledge, the application of this knowledge by the specific communities becomes more likely.

It is this vision of scholarship in the field of human development that is embodied in developmental systems perspectives such as developmental contextualism (Ford & Lerner, 1992; Miller & Lerner, 1994). Pursuing this vision, however, requires the integration of two cultures: the campus/faculty culture and the community culture. To address the problems of contemporary youth and families, universities and their faculties must seek legitimacy in both cultures (Boyer, 1994). A bridge must be created to bring the campus and the community together into a productive, colearning collaboration embodying the land-grant tradition. The key product produced by this collaboration is termed *outreach scholarship*.

OUTREACH SCHOLARSHIP

A means to envision the process involved in integrating the faculty and the community cultures is depicted in Figure 6.1. At the core of this process lies a commitment to outreach scholarship. In a report by the Michigan State University Provost's Committee on University Outreach (1993), outreach scholarship was defined as follows:

> The generation, transmission, application, and preservation of knowledge for the direct benefit of audiences to whom and for whom the university seeks to extend itself in ways that are consistent with university and unit missions. (p. 2)

This conception is quite congruent with the view of research embodied in the applied developmental science (ADS) perspective discussed in Chapter 3, that is, as the "systematic synthesis of research and application to describe, explain, and promote optimal developmental outcomes in individuals and families as they develop along the life cycle" (Fisher & Lerner, 1994, p. 4).

To promote outreach scholarship requires input from both the faculty and community cultures; it promotes collaboration and leads to colearning.

From the perspective of the campus, outreach scholarship must be multidisciplinary, given that the problems faced by communities are multifaceted and thus cut across the boundaries of any one disciplinary specialization. But, in addition, it is critical that such scholarship also simultaneously and synthetically try to be multicultural—in several senses of the word. Such scholarship must attempt to link the cultures of different professions; the cultures of different disciplines, departments, and colleges; the culture of the Cooperative Extension Service; the culture of the Agricultural Experimental Station; and the diverse cultures within the spectrum of communities that are constituted by the children and families served by the university.

Scholarship derived from such multicultural competence represents a new vision for the knowledge functions of a university, one that promises to embody the way in which a land-grant university can best position itself in the next century to respond to the multifaceted problems of the people it serves. To provide an overview of this vision, it is useful to discuss the components of Figure 6.1.

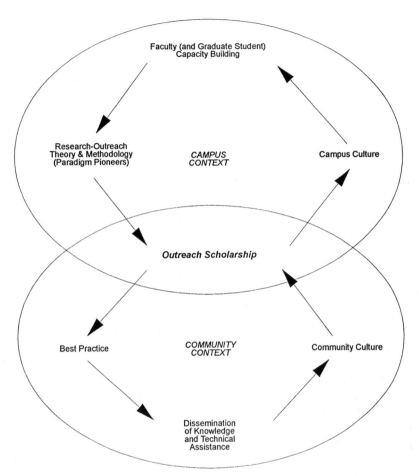

Figure 6.1. Changes in the campus and community context promoted by a developmental contextual view of the integration of research and outreach.

THE CAMPUS CONTEXT

As shown in the top half of Figure 6.1, outreach scholarship requires (a) a change in campus culture, (b) faculty/graduate student capacity building, and (c) the development of research-outreach theory and methodology.

Campus Culture

Schein (1992) defines organizational culture as

a pattern of basic assumptions that a given group has invented, discovered or developed in learning to cope with its problems of external adaptation and internal integration, and that has worked well enough to be considered valid, and therefore, to be taught to new members as the correct way to perceive, think, and feel in relation to those problems. (p. 12)

The campus culture provides meaning and context for faculty. It holds people together and provides both an individual and collective sense of purpose. Perhaps most important, the campus culture defines the nature of reality for those who are part of the culture.

The current campus culture—with its overemphasis on research for the sake of research—has placed research universities in trouble. As noted by Hackney (1991):

As the university has become more important to society, it is losing its special place it once held in the scheme of things. Knowledge has become much more central to society and to the economy, yet universities are increasingly pictured as just another snout at the public trough.

In this climate, a university must realize that it cannot take a business-as-usual approach (Boyer, 1994). The key to the success of any attempt at instituting a revised approach to the activities of the university rests on changing the campus culture. However, to discuss how I envision fostering such culture change, it is important to look at the two other components in the top half of Figure 6.1.

Faculty Capacity Building

Based on a developmental contextual conception of human development and on an ADS approach to research (i.e., on a developmental contextual conception of outreach scholarship), we must seek to build the capacity of faculty (and graduate students) to see the world as a system. The inculcation of this perspective may require helping faculty see beyond their disciplinary-based perspectives and aiding them in understanding the changing interrelations among levels of organization that comprise human systems. Although throughout this book I have stressed the developmental contextual approach to such systems, I believe that it is useful to remain open to any of the systems approaches comprising the "fifth discipline" (i.e., the use of systems concepts to promote organizational learning and development) (Senge, 1990; see also Levine & Fitzgerald, 1992).

Using a developmental systems perspective will allow a linkage among outreach scholarship, graduate education in ADS, and, as well, undergraduate service learning experiences related to ADS. The nature of this linkage is illustrated in Figure 6.2.

Integrating Theory and Methodology

A key feature of the developmental contextual approach to outreach scholarship is the integration of theory and methodology. Accordingly, to address adequately the serious problems faced by today's children, adolescents, and families, multidisciplinary research must involve more than just assembling researchers from different disciplines. Such an approach typically results in a simple layering of investigations and publications—project faculty from each discipline approach the topic with their own theory and method and report their findings separately or in an edited collection of articles.

Pursuing this traditional paradigm has built the scholarly careers of numerous generations of faculty. However, this paradigm is not adequate for meeting the needs of the youth and families of our communities. What is required is a pioneering effort to formulate a new paradigm promoting an integrative or, even better, fused and multicultural (in the above senses) approach to research.

The variables that various disciplines typically study, and the models that they develop to interrelate those variables, are all commingled in the day-to-day situations of real life. Only the building of integrated models that focus on the combined interactions of systems studied by different disciplines will allow the heretofore disconnected insights of those different disciplines to develop into a useful, synthetic theory guiding the development of policies and programs. The point is not simply the obvious one that the context is complex; rather it is that the fusing of distinct approaches requires building systemic, integrated, and dynamic models and methods.

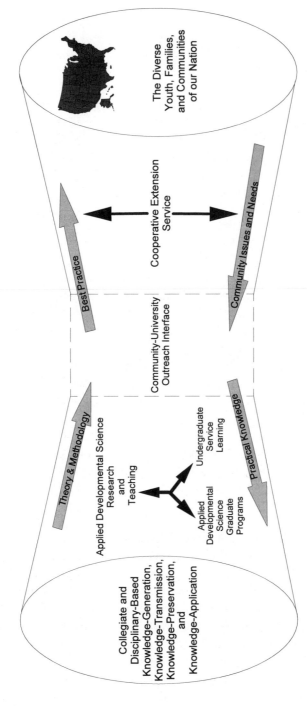

Figure 6.2. Research-extension collaborations integrating teaching, research, and outreach for the diverse youth, families, and communities of America.

To enable high-quality outreach scholarship derived from this systems perspective to be pursued productively requires innovative methodology. Such methods must be able to garner evidence that is both scientifically rigorous and persuasive to the faculty culture and relevant and compelling to the communities with whom we collaborate. As a consequence of our developmental systems perspective, the methodology that is promoted will be multivariate, longitudinal, and change sensitive.

There is one important implication that follows from this approach to methodology. Because of these methodological choices and, in particular, the commitment to the longitudinal approach, one must be involved in communities over a long period of time. This temporal commitment means, substantively, that activities associated with outreach scholarship will avoid the hit-and-run character of many prior attempts at action research, applied research, and demonstration projects. As implied above, I do not see as scientifically or ethically defensible scholarship that parachutes into a community and fails to grapple with (a) the long-term outcome of individual and family changes, (b) the status of the capacity of the community to sustain programmatic changes once the demonstration period has ended, or (c) the unintended consequences or new insights that arise during the period.

Campus Culture Change

To understand and effect these pioneering efforts requires a major qualitative change in the current culture of America's campuses (Boyer, 1994). However, it is important to emphasize that the involvement of faculty in such cultural change is no small task. Indeed, because there are still only a relatively few faculty at any institution involved with the type of multicultural integration I have described, one of the major activities within any university must be the building of teams of colleagues that exemplify the integrations that are embodied in the above-noted concept of campus cultural change. With this team, it is possible to begin to institutionalize and extend the diffusion of these innovations. To this end, I believe that the cycle in the top part of Figure 6.1 is synthetically reinforcing: Outreach scholarship will change the campus culture that, in turn, will lead to increases in the capacity of faculty and graduate students to conduct outreach scholarship that will lead to pioneering efforts to enhance theory and methodology.

Together, both the quality and quantity of outreach scholarship will increase as a consequence of these efforts. As well, the catalyzing of outreach
scholarship will facilitate efforts to collaborate within communities. At
this point, then, it is useful to review the bottom half of Figure 6.1.

THE COMMUNITY CONTEXT

As shown in the bottom half of Figure 6.1, outreach scholarship gener-
ates a knowledge base about best practice, and the knowledge base is disseminated through training and technical assistance. These activities
generate positive outcomes in the community, such that there is an increased likelihood that it will turn to the university for further collaborations involving outreach scholarship.

This process of community collaboration fosters a sense of community
that is at least as broad as the diverse settings and constituencies that influence the lives of children, adolescents, and families. Thus included in this
sense of community are geographical units (e.g., neighborhoods and mu-
nicipalities), institutional units (e.g., school districts and service agencies),
and governmental actors (e.g., elected and appointed officials). As well,
this process of community collaboration rests on colearning: Members of
the campus and the community contexts need to learn about each other's
culture for productive and effective outreach scholarship to result.

Thus commitment to scholarship predicated on colearning will create,
from the perspective of the community, a different type of academic research institution. Whereas other research institutions see the community
as a laboratory, a colearning conception sees the community as a class-
room in which both the university and community can learn. As such, involvement with communities is one of commingled destinies. Each
partner's success is interdependent with that of the other partner. This
mutuality means, then, that campus and community must become competent about the mores, values, and practices of each other's culture. Unless such cultural competence is developed, neither colearning nor
effective scholarly and community outcomes can be achieved.

It is here, then, in the establishment of effective systems of colearning,
that extension can play a vital role in the enhancement of integrating the
cultures of campus and community. As part of both communities, exten-

sion colleagues can enhance and facilitate within each setting under-standing of the meaning and value systems of the other setting—a role displayed in Figure 6.2. Enactment of this role will be crucial in the design, implementation, and evaluation of effective community-based programs for children and adolescents.

Research and Extension Collaborations
and the Development of Effective Community-Based Programs

Developmental contextualism stresses that the problems facing the youth of America require an integrated set of activities by the members of our nation's research and extension communities (Lerner & Miller, 1993). As emphasized in the scholarship of Dryfoos (1990), Hamburg (1992), and Schorr (1988), numerous programs have been empirically shown to be able to break the cycle of disadvantage (Schorr, 1988) and to prevent some of the sequelae of persistent and pervasive child and adolescent poverty (Dryfoos, 1990).

Yet, despite the presence of such evaluation data, I have noted that many of these demonstrably effective programs have not been sustained (Schorr, 1988). Even fewer have been replicated. The problems of sustainability and replicability are interrelated, and the potentially integrated role of members of the research and extension communities arises in connection to this interrelation.

As discussed above, effective programs for youth have often not been sustained because members of the community within which the program is embedded do not have the capacity themselves to maintain the program. With no attempt to empower the youth or other members of the community to sustain the program over the long term, any salutary outcomes of the program are likely to fade out. Thus what needs to be ascertained is how—*for a specific program in a particular community*—can such capacity be developed? More specifically, what needs to be asked is,

- How can the members of a given community, and particularly the youth who are involved in the program, be provided with the leadership abilities to sustain the program after the term of the demonstration project (or grant) has ended?
- What set of developmental skills, and what array of community, political, and economic leadership abilities, need to be inculcated in these youth to enhance their capacity and, as a result, that of their community?

Research and extension go hand in hand in what are clearly youth development endeavors. Once researchers provide answers to these questions, either new programs and/or adjuncts to existing programs need to be devised to turn these answers into changed outcomes, that is, into increased leadership capacity, for the youth of a specific community. Furthermore, the capacity-building programs or program supplements need to be evaluated for their effectiveness, *and* the knowledge about one community and its programs needs to be adjusted for applicability to (i.e., replicability in) any other community. As a consequence, the partnership between research and extension needs to encompass understanding of, and programs for, both sustaining effective efforts in any one community and replicating such efforts in other communities (cf. Lerner, 1993a; Lerner & Miller, 1993).

From Replication to Building the Best Practice

From the perspective of the members of a community, the value of outreach scholarship is that it results in knowledge of the best practices available to them for policies, policy implementation, and program design and delivery in their neighborhoods. As noted by Washington (1992):

> Dozens of effective strategies have been used across the country to address the needs of youth and families. Yet in all areas of social development there is the temptation to start over again rather than build on efforts already underway and proven successful. . . . The time has come to focus on less glamorous, self aggrandizing aspects of program development. Instead, professional communities need to cooperate more to leverage their collective investments and establish comprehensive, coordinated policies and practices that work efficiently and effectively.
>
> To avoid the temptation of starting over again, better systems for documenting what has been done and providing a clearinghouse for the information are needed. In addition, there is a need for development of a reporting and rating system for social development efforts that would help successful models that have been developed locally to be highlighted and shared nationally.
>
> University faculty, through their research and evaluation activities, can give important leadership to helping design appropriate techniques to learn and transfer information about "what works."

The sort of information called for by Washington (1992) would include programs that have been developed, implemented, and evaluated all over the world (cf. Little, 1993). This information may allow public policymakers, community organizers, researchers, and others to better use their money and time developing or replicating successful programs. Many people within these groups know there are programs that succeed in improving the life chances of America's children, adolescents, and families. As emphasized eloquently and often by Edelman (1993) and by Little (1993), we have a good deal of the knowledge and the skills needed to design and deliver programs that ameliorate undesirable behaviors, prevent the occurrence of problems, and enhance the abilities and life opportunities for the diverse youth and families across our nation.

Simply, there are ways to construct the contexts of youth that enhance the development of youth across the life span and do not squander their human capital. Indeed, many of these programs, and the policies and values that legitimate and promote them, have been identified by Hamburg (1992), Schorr (1988), and Dryfoos (1990, 1994). However, despite the proven successes of selected programs—often documented through the results of rigorous evaluations—these programs are neither sufficiently sustained nor adequately replicated. A failure to replicate, or more primarily to disseminate the details of successful programs so that replication can be attempted, means that practitioners in different communities must "reinvent the wheel." Best practice cannot be identified if replication does not exist. More primarily, however, even when a community finds that a program works, it is often not sustained because there is a lack of community-based capacity to generate requisite leadership, infrastructure, and funds (Schorr, 1988).

The need exists, then, to catalog information about what works in specific communities in regard to preventive, enhancing, or ameliorative programs for children, adolescents, and families. Of course, best practice is an ideal that can only be approached, especially given the fact that the developmental contextualism model indicates that particular instances of individual and ecological relations may not generalize precisely to different individual or contextual conditions (Lerner, 1986). Thus work here is more readily characterized as the pursuing of "better practice." Nevertheless, we need to disseminate best (or at least, better) practice information to inform communities and policymakers about the sorts of programs that may work and about how programs that have been sustained have managed to achieve this end. Moreover, dissemination is required to increase the capacity of the community itself to sustain activities beyond the period of university collaboration.

Dissemination of Knowledge and Technical Assistance

To translate research-extension collaborations into community-based programs that are marked by the capacity of the people of the community themselves to sustain the programs, research-extension teams must be proactive about disseminating knowledge and providing technical assistance. Simply, this approach not only helps to extend and sustain identified best practices but also assists in building the capacities of community collaborators. As colearning members, the research and extension colleagues would initiate the delivery, to their community collaborators, of knowledge about and skills for enhancing the lives of children, adolescents, and families.

The knowledge valued and sought by the research-extension-community partnership must be usable and used. As a consequence, key facets of the developmental systems approach to dissemination and technical assistance involve ascertaining the relevance of knowledge and assuring accessibility to it. This view of knowledge application underscores the need for a sustained commitment to a campus-community partnership. If such partnerships are successful, they will build the understanding of universities as a potential part of a confederation of community members, a partnership that brings to the "collaborative table" knowledge-based assets. In this way, the community can also be proactive in approaching the university. These approaches can help further attempts by research and extension colleagues to learn with the community the means to refine the outreach scholarship being pursued and further the inculcation of best practices that meet the specific needs of the community, which will, as a consequence, help to merge the cultures of the campus and the community.

Community Culture

If the university's efforts at pioneering a new paradigm for outreach scholarship are effective in the community, then the community will alter the way it views its problems, the policy choices it pursues, the programs to which it subscribes, and perhaps superordinately, the university-based resources it perceives it can access for making these changes. In other words, if community culture change occurs, then the view of the role of the university will also change.

These alterations are a key goal of pursuing outreach scholarship within the frame provided by developmental contextualism. A hope is that legislative and community leaders will recognize that funds expended on the university-community relationship constitute a productive invest-ment, one that has a tangible return in regard to the issues and problems they define as crucial. Moreover, as Little (1993) believes, if such systems change is useful in one community context, then it may be possible to cre-ate economies of scale: Building better practices in one setting may teach us how to extend our efforts to other settings, to other parts of the ecology of human development. As a consequence, the developmental approach to colearning and to community collaboration may help facilitate the devel-opment of systems thinking among policymakers, program professionals, volunteers, and the children and families involved in the outreach scholar-ship collaboration.

CONCLUSIONS

Current findings from research and program evaluation efforts perti-nent to attempts to prevent the problems of children and adolescents en-courage researchers and extension leaders to pursue collaborative youth development efforts. By together learning how to build the capacity of the youth of our communities to take leadership in sustaining effective pre-vention and enhancement programs, the research and extension commu-nities can together aid American universities in making substantial contributions to ending the destruction of our nation's youth. Indeed, col-laborations of research and extension colleagues can help move beyond just the deterrence of problems; these collaborations can help build better lives for the children and adolescents of our nation (Pittman & Zeldin, 1994).

However, to better enable research and extension to collaborate effec-tively in the design, delivery, replication, and evaluation of youth develop-ment programs will require substantial revisions in existing social policies

pertinent to America's children and adolescents. Moreover, academic policies that currently inhibit research and extension collaborations will need
to be revised if universities are to be institutions involved in the solution
of the problems of our nation's youth. It is important to specify, then, the
academic and social policy innovations that need to be introduced to allow the research and extension communities to build and sustain effective
programs for the youth of our nation.

7

Implications for
Social and Academic Policy

Policies represent standards, or rules, for the conduct of individuals, organizations, and institutions. The policies we formulate and follow structure our actions and let others know how they may expect us to function in regard to the substantive issues to which our policies pertain. Moreover, policies reflect what we value, what we believe, and what we think is in our best interests; policies indicate the things in which we are invested and about which we care.

Today, all too many Americans do not see the need for a comprehensive and integrated national policy pertinent to all of our nation's children. To the contrary, many Americans see youth problems as associated with other people's children. Their stereotyped image of the at-risk or poor child is of a minority youth living in the inner city. Yet the probability that an American child or adolescent will be poor—and thus experience the several rotten outcomes (Schorr, 1988) of poverty—does not differ in regard to whether that youth lives in an urban or a rural setting (Huston, 1992). Moreover, the incidence of risk behaviors among our nation's youth (Dryfoos, 1990, 1994) extends the problems of America's children and adolescents far beyond the bounds associated with the numbers of our nation's poor or minority children.

For these reasons alone, there appears to be ample reason for the development of a national youth policy pertinent to all of America's children and adolescents. However, there are additional reasons. Just as we may be concerned with developing better policies for sustaining and/or enhancing American agricultural, industrial, manufacturing, and business interests, it would seem clear that we must not lose sight of the need to sustain the communities—and the people—involved in the production, distribution, *and* the consumption of the products of our economy.

Still, we often neglect the fact that problems of rural and urban youth—problems that are similarly structured, similarly debilitating, and similarly destructive of America's human capital—diminish significantly our nation's present and future ability to sustain and enhance our nation's economic productivity. Clearly, then, both from the standpoint of the problems of children and adolescents and from the perspective of enlightened self-interest within America's industrial, agricultural, business, and consumer communities, policies need to be directed to enhancing youth development, to preventing the loss of human capital associated with the breadth and depth of the problems confronting our children and adolescents.

TOWARD THE DEVELOPMENT
OF A NATIONAL YOUTH POLICY

Yet, despite the historically unprecedented growth in the magnitude of the problems of America's youth and of the contextual conditions that exacerbate these problems (e.g., changes in family structure and function and in child and adolescent poverty rates), there have been few major policy initiatives taken to address these increasingly more direly changing circumstances. Indeed, as Hamburg (1992) has noted:

> During the past three decades, as all these remarkable changes increasingly jeopardized healthy child development, the nation took little notice. One arcane but important manifestation of this neglect was the low research priority and inadequate science policy for this field. As a result, the nature of this new generation of problems was poorly understood; emerging trends were insufficiently recognized; and authority tended to substitute for evidence, and ideology for analysis. Until the past few years, political, business, and professional leaders had very little to say about the problems of children and youth. Presidents have tended to pass the responsibility to the states and the private sector. State leaders often passed the responsibility

back to the federal government on the one hand or over to the cities on the other. And so it goes. (p. 13)

As a result of this "treatment" of social policy regarding our nation's children and adolescents, the United States has no national youth policy per se (Hahn, 1994). Rather, policies and the programs associated with them tend to be focused on the family (e.g., Aid for Dependent Children, AFDC) and not on youth per se (Huston, 1992). As such, although these policies may influence the financial status of the family, they may not readily impact on, and certainly they fail to emphasize, youth development. That is, these policies do not focus on the enhancement of the capacities and the potentials of America's children and adolescents. For instance, a policy or program that provides a job for an unemployed single mother but results in the placement of her child in an inadequate day care environment for extended periods of time may enhance the financial resources of the family; however, it may do so at the cost of placing the child in an unstimulating and, possibly, detrimental environment.

Accordingly, if we are to substantially reduce the current waste of human life and potential caused by the problems confronting contemporary American youth, new policy options must be pursued, ones that focus on children and adolescents and emphasize positive youth development and not only amelioration, remediation, and/or deterrence of problems. Thus, as recently argued by Pittman and Zeldin (1994), "The reduction of problem behaviors among young people is a necessary policy goal. But it is not enough. We must be equally committed to articulating and nurturing those attributes that we wish adolescents to develop and demonstrate" (p. 53). Based on this perspective, Pittman and Zeldin forward several policy recommendations that, in their combination, provide a means to develop a national youth policy supportive of the positive development of children and adolescents.

First, given their above-noted perspective, Pittman and Zeldin (1994) emphasize that policy must focus on youth development, and not on deterrence. Resources must be provided to ascertain the competencies and potentials of youth and to develop and evaluate programs designed to promote these positive attributes.

The support of research about, and programs for, positive youth development leads to a second policy recommendation forwarded by Pittman and Zeldin (1994), one acknowledging the crucial role played by youth-serving organizations in enhancing the life chances of youth (cf. Carnegie Corporation of New York, 1992; Dryfoos, 1990; National Research Council, 1993; Schorr, 1988). That is, policies must promote the financial support and broad acceptance of community-based youth organizations; such acceptance involves support of the socialization experiences and youth services provided by these organizations.

However, to promote the acceptance of community programs, another policy step must be taken: "The policy goal of facilitating youth development must be translated and incorporated into the public institutions of education, employment and training, juvenile justice, and health services" (Pittman & Zeldin, 1994, p. 53). The translation involved in this policy step is based on the view that the promotion of youth development is not the exclusive province of any single organization or agency, a view emphasized by Dryfoos (1990), Schorr (1988), and Hamburg (1992). To the contrary, then, an integrated, community-wide effort is necessary to foster positive youth development (Dryfoos, 1990; Hamburg, 1992; Schorr, 1988). Hamburg (1992) makes a similar point. He suggests three policy initiatives that, together, would enhance the capacity of communities to (a) provide comprehensive and integrated services that (b) promoted positive youth development through (c) the provision of effective programs delivered by a well-trained staff. Thus Hamburg (1992) notes that he would:

> First, use federal and state mechanisms to provide funding to local communities in ways that encourage the provision of coherent, comprehensive services. State and federal funding should provide incentives to encourage collaboration and should be adaptable to local circumstances.
>
> Second, provide training programs to equip professional staff and managers with the necessary skills. Such programs would include training for collaboration among professionals in health, mental health, education, and social services, and would instill a respectful, sensitive attitude toward working with clients, patients, parents, and students from different backgrounds.
>
> Three, use widespread evaluation to determine what intervention is useful for whom, how funds are being spent, and whether the services are altogether useful. (p. 166)

Thus policy must move from a focus on just building effective programs to also building cohesive and effective communities (National Research Council, 1993; Pittman & Zeldin, 1994). Indeed, a recent report by the National Research Council (1993) notes that building supportive communities for youth faced with the destruction of their life chances "will require a major commitment from federal and state governments and the private sector, including support for housing, transportation, economic development, and the social services required by poor and low-income residents" (p. 239).

Finally, Pittman and Zeldin (1994) emphasize that for youth development programs to attain sustained successes—across the span of individual lives and across multiple generations—issues of individual and economic diversity must be clearly and directly confronted. Specifically, poverty and racism must be a continued, core focus of social policy. We must continue to be vigilant about the pernicious sequelae of poverty among children and adolescents, about the vast overrepresentation of minority youth among the ranks of our nation's poor, and about the greater probability that minority youth will be involved in the several problem behaviors besetting their generation.

In sum, then, the policy recommendations forwarded by Pittman and Zeldin (1994), Hamburg (1992), and the National Research Council (1993) stress the importance of comprehensive and integrative actions involving both proximal community participation and the contributions of broader segments of the public and private sectors, community-based evaluations, diversity, and promoting positive development across the life span. As may be recognized from a review of the presentations in preceding chapters, these ideas are consistent with those brought to the fore by a developmental contextual perspective.

Indeed, throughout this book, I have forwarded developmental contextualism as a useful means for pursuing outreach scholarship pertinent to the issues of health and development facing today's children, adolescents, families, and communities. I have argued that, from the perspective of developmental contextualism, policies—and the programs that do (or should) derive from them—merge (or, better, synthesize) basic and applied research. That is, policies and programs represent the means through which ecologically valid interventions may be enacted; evaluation of these interventions provides information, then, about both the adequacy of these applied endeavors and the basic theoretical issues of human development—about bases for the enhancement of the life courses of individuals, families, and communities (Lerner & Miller, 1993; Lerner et al., 1994).

Thus, from the perspective of developmental contextualism, policies and the evaluation of their influences or outcomes are actions that allow outreach scholars to make contributions to the understanding of, and to service to, the diverse children, adolescents, and families of our nation. However, developmental contextualism provides more than a structure for the integration of basic and applied scholarship; it offers more than a frame for viewing policy engagement and programming as the methods for this integration, for the enactment of applied developmental science (ADS) (Fisher & Lerner, 1994). In addition, there are several substantive directions for the development of policies pertinent to the youth of America that are promoted by developmental contextualism. It is useful to discuss them.

IMPLICATIONS OF DEVELOPMENTAL
CONTEXTUALISM FOR YOUTH POLICY

There are at least six substantive foci of youth policy that may be derived from a developmental contextual perspective. The first is associated with the fact that developmental contextualism promotes an emphasis on the developmental system (Ford & Lerner, 1992). Within this system, development involves changes in *relations* between the growing person and his or her context (Lerner, 1991). Accordingly, to enhance development, to promote positive youth development, we must focus our efforts on this system, and not on either the individual (cf. Dryfoos, 1990; Schorr, 1988) or the context per se. As such, policies should be aimed at building programs that enhance *relationships* for youth across the breadth of the system, that is, with family members, peers, schools, and indeed across institutions of the proximal community and the more distal society.

Second, we must recognize that the system within which both youth and the programs aimed at them are embedded is also the system that contains the institutions that do (or could) provide resources for the promotion of youth and program development. Accordingly, we should use the multiple connections within the developmental system to create innovative approaches to generating resources to design, deliver, evaluate, and sustain effective youth-serving programs.

An example of the potential of such innovation is provided by Little (1993). He notes that all too often programs that might have a chance of being effective are not implemented or sustained. Little believes that one of the key reasons for this situation is that the procedure that has been used to secure program funding is not effective. That is, Little (1993) notes that whereas people with ideas start programs, often at a grassroots level, they typically have to go to a person with institutional power (e.g., a supervisor or a director/president of an organization) to find a potential advocate for the idea of the program. In turn, then, if this person with institutional power is persuaded to be an advocate for the program, he or she would (because of his or her role) be in a position to approach yet another person, someone with authority over resources (e.g., a program officer of a community foundation), to secure resources for the program. This procedure is, at best, only intermittently successful, and as such, Little (1993) believes it represents a weak link in the system through which program funding occurs. Accordingly, he recommends that new linkages be formed in the system, ones between people of influence (i.e., those with control over resources) and people of ideas.

For instance, the International Youth Foundation promotes direct involvement of program officers from indigenous, grant-making, community foundations with the communities and the programs that they fund. This systems change represents an important paradigm shift in the nature of the process involved in funding community-based youth programs.

A third policy implication for youth programs that is associated with developmental contextualism also is derived from an understanding of the developmental system within which young people are embedded: A system that is open to change for the better is also open to change for the worse. Accordingly, to effect sustained enhancement of the lives of youth, we need policies that promote long-term interventions. A one-shot intervention will not "inoculate" a youth for life against the potentially risk-actualizing perturbations of the developmental system within which he or she continues to live. Thus we need to build (and fund) long-term—that is, life-span-oriented—convoys of social support (Kahn & Antonucci, 1980) to reinforce and further the positive developments that may accrue from effective youth programs.

The life-span nature of the developmental system within which youth are embedded is associated with a fourth implication for the development of policy. Transitions occur across the life span (Lerner & Spanier, 1980), and often, these changes are qualitative in nature.

For example, the transitions involved in the period between childhood and early adolescence involve qualitative alterations in thinking abilities (i.e., formal operational ability emerges) (Piaget, 1960, 1972), emotions and personality (e.g., involving the psychosocial crisis of identity versus role confusions) (Erikson, 1959), social relationships (e.g., a shift in primary social group—from parents to peers—occurs) (Guerney & Arthur, 1984), and physiology (i.e., a new—sexual—drive and new hormones emerge during this period) (A. Freud, 1969; Katchadourian, 1977). Given such qualitative changes, a program that provides a goodness of fit (Lerner & Lerner, 1989; Thomas & Chess, 1977) with the characteristics of the person during childhood may not continue to be fit during adolescence. Accordingly, to be sure that the features of our programs remain qualitatively valid across the life span, we must monitor and calibrate our programs to attend to developmental changes and, as well, to contextual transitions (for example, involving the shift from elementary schools to middle or junior high schools) (Simmons & Blyth, 1987).

A fifth policy implication, one closely related to the idea of transitions across life, pertains to the issue of individual differences (diversity) and of transformations of individuals and contexts. Developmental contextualism stresses that diversity—of individuals, contexts (including cultural ones), and individual-context relations—is the rule of human behavior and development. "One size," that is, one type of intervention, "does not fit all." Policies and programs that are fit and effective for youth of one social, racial, ethnic, community, or cultural group may be irrelevant, poorly suited, or even damaging to youth with other characteristics of individuality. As such, policies and programs must be sensitive to the instances of human diversity relevant to the community or group to which they are directed and organized to provide a goodness of fit.

However, it will not be sufficient just to have policies that promote the development of diversity-sensitive programs. Such policies must promote as well a continuing awareness that individual differences *increase* as people develop across their life spans (Baltes, 1987; Schaie, 1979); as such, we must enable programs to be adjusted to fit the transformations in the character of individuality that emerge across life.

For instance, each human, as he or she develops across life, becomes increasingly different from other people as a consequence of his or her individual history of experiences, roles, and relationships (Lerner, 1988; Lerner & Tubman, 1989). Thus initial characteristics of individuality are continually transformed over the course of life into different instances of individuality. As a consequence of such transformations in individuality, we must develop programs that are attentive to both initial and to emergent characteristics of individuality—of the person, context, and especially, person-context relations.

The stress on individuality within developmental contextualism leads to a final implication for youth policy, one that returns us to the point that the outreach scholarship promoted by this perspective involves a merger of both basic and applied science. Developmental contextualism conceives of evaluation as providing information both about policy and program efficacy and about how the course of human development can be enhanced through policies and programs. Indeed, because the DICE procedures promoted by developmental contextualism (Lerner et al., in press; Ostrom et al., 1994) involve the active participation of the individuals served by the program (Weiss & Greene, 1992), evaluation is also a means to empower program participants and to enhance their capacities to engage in actions (i.e., program design, delivery, and evaluation) that promote their own positive development.

Accordingly, policies should promote the use of participatory-normative evaluation procedures (Weiss & Greene, 1992), such as those associated with the DICE model. Such evaluations will increase understanding of the lives developing within the context of the policies and programs one is implementing and, simultaneously, will inculcate greater capacities and thus further empower the youth, families, and communities involved in the programs that are being evaluated.

The important role that participatory evaluation procedures can play within a developmental contextual approach to youth policy raises, once again (e.g., see Chapter 6), the issue of the potential contributions of academe and of academicians to addressing the problems facing America's youth. However, if our nation's universities are to be a part of enacting effective community coalitions and fostering continued development of an integrative and comprehensive national youth policy addressing the needs of America's youth, social policy innovations must be coupled with alterations in academic policies and practices. Without such changes in the academy, our nation's universities will not be able to be integral participants in addressing the needs of our country's children and adolescents. It is important, then, to discuss some of the academic policy changes that may need to be introduced for such participation to occur.

DIMENSIONS OF ACADEMIC POLICY CHANGE

American universities cannot become effective parts of the solution to the problems besetting our nation's youth until increased numbers of researcher and extension colleagues begin to work collaboratively, both among themselves and with the communities they serve. To bring researchers into this collaboration will not only require the cultural changes discussed in Chapter 6. In addition, and arguably primarily, the reward systems of American universities will have to be altered (Boyer, 1990, 1994; Lerner et al., 1994; Votruba, 1992). Incentives will need to be created that provide an exciting and attractive basis for the reorientation of the work of established scholars and for the reward of a career in outreach scholarship among junior faculty. In addition, educators in each discipline involved in the study of human development should be presented with a vision for beginning to train their students differently (Birkel, Lerner, & Smyer, 1989; Fisher et al., 1993). An appreciation of systematic change, context, and human relationships should be the cornerstone of future graduate education.

These emphases are central points stressed in the growing attention being paid among scholarly societies and universities to the importance of training in ADS for future scholars and professionals in fields associated with human development and education (Fisher & Lerner, 1994; Fisher et al., 1993). We should instill in these future scholars and professionals a greater appreciation of the importance of interindividual differences in the timing of causal, dynamic interactions—for the development of human diversity and for the contextual variation that is both a product and a producer of it (Lerner, 1982; Lerner & Busch-Rossnagel, 1981).

Furthermore, it is crucial that university merit, tenure, and promotion committees evaluating scientists studying development be urged to begin to consider the relative value of multidisciplinary collaborative, and hence multiauthored, publications, in comparison to within-discipline, single-authored products. Academic policy discussion must also involve the nature of the reception given by university review committees to the sort of contextual and collaborative research associated with developmental systems approaches to outreach scholarship. The issue to be debated here is whether we can train future cohorts of applied developmental scientists to engage productively in the multidisciplinary, multiprofessional, and community collaborations requisite for advancing understanding of the basic process of development and then not reward and value them (e.g., tenure and promote them) for successfully doing so.

If we follow a developmental contextual perspective that leads to the synthesis of science and outreach, then it would seem that we must devise means to assign value to and reward an array of collaborative, multidisciplinary, and multiprofessional activities (Votruba, 1992). Similarly, if we are to take seriously the need for change-oriented (and hence longitudinal), multilevel (and hence multivariate), and multidisciplinary research, we must recognize the need to educate government agencies and private foundations about the time and financial resources that should be given to such collaborative activities (McLoyd, 1994).

Simply, American universities must do more than provide a model for the integration of multiple academic disciplines and multiple professional activities with the community. They must embrace fully—by rewarding behavior consistent with—the ideal of multidimensional excellence, that is, of high-quality contributions across the breadth of the academic missions of research, teaching, and outreach. In other words, if universities are to significantly advance the integration of science and outreach for the diverse children, adolescents, and families of America's communities, sustained efforts must be made to build and maintain—through a revised academic reward system—a new, community-collaborative scholarly agenda.

This is the key challenge facing American universities as our nation approaches the next millennium (Boyer, 1994). And this is the path on which we—as scholars, educators, youth-serving professionals, volunteers, and most basically, citizens—must embark. Indeed, as I noted at the outset, the stakes are high, not only for universities but, more important, for an American society faced with the loss of much of the human capital represented by its children and adolescents. This observation leads to some final comments.

CONCLUSIONS

Ultimately, we must all continue to educate ourselves about the best means available to promote enhanced life chances among all of our youth, but especially those whose potentials for positive contributions to our nation are most in danger of being wasted (Lerner, 1993a). The collaborative expertise of the research and extension communities can provide much of this information, especially if it obtained in partnership with strong, empowered communities. Policies promoting such coalitions will be an integral component of a national youth development policy aimed at creating caring communities having the capacity to nurture the healthy development of our children and adolescents.

There is no time to lose in the development of such policies. America as we know it—and, even more, as we believe it can be—will be lost unless we act now. All the strengths and assets of our universities, of all of our institutions, and of all of our people must be marshaled for this effort.

The agenda is clear and the means to achieve it appear available. We need only the will. And this motivation will manifest itself when Americans recognize the validity of the point made by Marian Wright Edelman (1992), President of the Children's Defense Fund:

> In the waning years of the twentieth century, doing what is right for children and doing what is necessary to save our national economic skin have converged. (p. 93)

Let us work together to save our children, to save our families and communities, and—superordinately—to save America.

References

Ahlburg, D. A., & De Vita, C. J. (1992). New realities of the American family. *Population Bulletin, 47*(2), 1-44.

Allison, K. W. (1993). Adolescents living in "non-family" and alternative settings. In R. M. Lerner (Ed.), *Early adolescence: Perspectives on research, policy, and intervention* (pp. 37-50). Hillsdale, NJ: Lawrence Erlbaum.

Allison, K. W., & Lerner, R. M. (1993). Integrating research, policy, and programs for adolescents and their families. In R. M. Lerner (Ed.), *Early adolescence: Perspectives on research, policy, and intervention* (pp. 17-23). Hillsdale, NJ: Lawrence Erlbaum.

Alvarez, B. (in press). Assessing youth programs: An international perspective. *Comparative Education Review.*

Ames, C., & Ames, R. (Eds.). (1989). *Research in motivation in education: Vol. 3. Goals and cognitions.* New York: Academic Press.

Anastasi, A. (1958). Heredity, environment, and the question, "how?" *Psychological Review, 65,* 197-208.

Baca Zinn, M., & Eitzen, D. S. (1993). *Diversity in families* (3rd ed.). New York: HarperCollins College.

Baltes, P. B. (1968). Longitudinal and cross-sectional sequences in the study of age and generation effects. *Human Development, 11,* 145-171.

Baltes, P. B. (1987). Theoretical propositions of life-span developmental psychology: On the dynamics between growth and decline. *Developmental Psychology, 23,* 611-626.

Baltes, P. B., & Baltes, M. M. (1980). Plasticity and variability in psychological aging: Methodological and theoretical issues. In G. E. Gurski (Ed.), *Determining the effects of aging on the central nervous system* (pp. 41-66). Berlin: Schering.

Baltes, P. B., Dittmann-Kohli, F., & Dixon, R. A. (1984). New perspectives on the development of intelligence in adulthood: Toward a dual-process conception and model of selective optimization with compensation. In P. B. Baltes & O. G. Brim, Jr. (Eds.), *Life-span development and behavior* (Vol. 6, pp. 33-76). New York: Academic Press.

Baltes, P. B., Reese, H. W., & Lipsitt, L. P. (1980). Life-span developmental psychology. *Annual Review of Psychology, 31,* 65-110.

Baltes, P. B., Smith, J., & Staudinger, U. M. (1992). Wisdom and successful aging. In T. B. Sonderegger (Ed.), *Nebraska symposium on motivation* (Vol. 39, pp. 123-167). Lincoln: University of Nebraska Press.

Barringer, F. (1991, March 11). Census shows profound change in racial makeup of the nation. *The New York Times,* pp. 1, A12.

Bell, R. Q. (1968). A reinterpretation of the direction of effects in studies of socialization. *Psychological Review, 75,* 81-95.

Belsky, J., Lerner, R. M., & Spanier, G. B. (1984). *The child in the family.* Reading, MA: Addison-Wesley.

Birkel, R., Lerner, R. M., & Smyer, M. A. (1989). Applied developmental psychology as an implementation of a life-span view of human development. *Journal of Applied Developmental Psychology, 10,* 425-445.

Block, J. (1971). *Lives through time.* Berkeley, CA: Bancroft.

Bonnen, J. T. (1993). Reflections on the land-grant idea. In *Agriculture staff papers* (pp. 93-98). East Lansing: Michigan State University, College of Agriculture and Natural Resources.

Bornstein, M. H., & Tamis-LeMonda, C. S. (1990). Activities and interactions of mothers and their firstborn infants in the first six months of life: Covariation, stability, continuity, correspondence, and prediction. *Child Development, 61,* 1206-1217.

Bornstein, M. H., Tamis-LeMonda, C. S., Tal, J., Ludemann, P., Toda, S., Rahn, C. W., Pêcheux, M. G., Azuma, H., & Vardi, D. (1992). Maternal responsiveness to infants in three societies: The United States, France, and Japan. *Child Development, 63,* 808-821.

Boyer, E. L. (1990). *Scholarship reconsidered: Priorities of the professoriate.* Princeton, NJ: The Carnegie Foundation for the Advancement of Teaching.

Boyer, E. L. (1994, March 9). Creating the new American college [Point of View column]. *The Chronicle of Higher Education,* p. A48.

Brazelton, T. B., Koslowski, B., & Main, M. (1974). The origins of reciprocity: The early mother-infant interaction. In M. Lewis & L. A. Rosenblum (Eds.), *The effect of the infant on its caregivers.* New York: Wiley.

Brim, O. G., Jr., & Kagan, J. (Eds.). (1980). *Constancy and change in human development.* Cambridge, MA: Harvard University Press.

Bronfenbrenner, U. (1974). Developmental research, public policy, and the ecology of childhood. *Child Development, 45,* 1-5.

Bronfenbrenner, U. (1977). Toward an experimental ecology of human development. *American Psychologist, 32,* 513-531.

Bronfenbrenner, U. (1979). *The ecology of human development.* Cambridge, MA: Harvard University Press.

Bronfenbrenner, U. (1983). The context of development and the development of context. In R. M. Lerner (Ed.), *Developmental psychology: Historical and philosophical perspectives* (pp. 39-83). Hillsdale, NJ: Lawrence Erlbaum.

Bronfenbrenner, U., & Crouter, A. C. (1983). The evolution of environmental models in developmental research. In W. Kersen (Ed.), *Handbook of child psychology, Vol. 1: History, theories, and methods* (pp. 39-83). New York: Wiley.

Bubolz, M., & Sontag, M. S. (1993). Human ecology theory. In P. Boss, W. Doherty, R. LaRossa, W. Schumm, & S. Steinmetz (Eds.), *Sourcebook of family theories and methods: A contextual approach* (pp. 419-448). New York: Plenum.

Carnegie Corporation of New York. (1992, December). *A matter of time: Risk and opportunity in the nonschool hours.* (Available from Carnegie Council on Adolescent Development, P.O. Box 753, Waldorf, MD 20604)

Carnegie Corporation of New York. (1994, April). *Starting points: Meeting the needs of our youngest children.* (Available from Carnegie Corporation of New York, P.O. Box 753, Waldorf, MD 20604)

Carnegie Council on Adolescent Development. (1989). *Turning points: Preparing American youth for the 21st century.* (Available from Carnegie Council on Adolescent Development, 11 Dupont Circle, N.W., Washington, DC 20036)

Center for the Study of Social Policy. (1992). *Kids Count data book.* Washington, DC: Author.

Center for the Study of Social Policy. (1993). *Kids Count data book.* Washington, DC: Author.

Chess, S., & Thomas, A. (1984). *The origins and evolution of behavior disorders: Infancy to early adult life.* New York: Brunner/Mazel.

Children's Defense Fund. (1992). *Child poverty up nationally and in 33 states.* Washington, DC: Author.

Clarke, A. M., & Clarke, A.D.B. (Eds.). (1976). *Early experience: Myth and evidence.* New York: Free Press.

Comer, J. (1989). Educating poor minority children. *Scientific American, 259*(5), 42-48.

Cronbach, L., and Associates. (1980). *Toward reform of program evaluation.* San Francisco: Jossey-Bass.

Dixon, R. A., & Lerner, R. M. (1992). A history of systems in developmental psychology. In M. H. Bornstein & M. E. Lamb (Eds.), *Developmental psychology: An advanced textbook* (3rd ed., pp. 3-58). Hillsdale, NJ: Lawrence Erlbaum.

Dixon, R. A., Lerner, R. M., & Hultsch, D. F. (1991). The concept of development in individual and social change. In P. Van Geert & L. P. Mos (Eds.), *Annals of theoretical psychology* (Vol. 7, pp. 279-323). New York: Plenum.

Dryfoos, J. G. (1990). *Adolescents at risk: Prevalence and prevention.* New York: Oxford University Press.

Dryfoos, J. G. (1994). *Full service schools: A revolution in health and social services for children, youth and families.* San Fransico: Jossey-Bass.

Dryfoos, J. G. (in press). Full service schools: Revolution or fad? *Journal of Research on Adolescence.*

Duncan, G. J. (1992). The economic environment of childhood. In A. C. Huston (Ed.), *Children in poverty: Child development and public policy* (pp. 23-50). Cambridge, UK: Cambridge University Press.

Eccles, J. S., & Midgley, C. (1989). Stage-environment fit: Developmentally appropriate classrooms for young adolescents. In C. Ames & R. Ames (Eds.), *Research in motivation in education: Vol. 3. Goals and cognitions* (pp. 139-186). New York: Academic Press.

Edelman, M. W. (1992). *The measure of our success: A letter to my children and yours.* Boston: Beacon Press.

Edelman, M. W. (1993, March). *Leave no child behind: Mobilizing families and communities for America's children.* Annual national conference of the Children's Defense Fund. Washington, DC: Children's Defense Fund.

Elder, G. H., Jr. (1974). *Children of the Great Depression: Social change in life experiences.* Chicago: University of Chicago Press.

Elder, G. H., Jr. (1980). Adolescence in historical perspective. In J. Adelson (Ed.), *Handbooks of adolescent psychology* (pp. 3-46). New York: Wiley.

Elder, G. H., Jr., Modell, J., & Parke, R. D. (1993). Studying children in a changing world. In G. H. Elder, Jr., J. Modell, & R. D. Parke (Eds.), *Children in time and place: Developmental and historical insights* (pp. 3-21). New York: Cambridge University Press.

Enarson, H. L. (1989). *Revitalizing the landgrant mission.* Blacksburg: Virginia Polytechnic Institute and State University Press.

Erikson, E. H. (1950). *Childhood and society*. New York: Norton.

Erikson, E. H. (1959). Identity and the life-cycle. *Psychological Issues, 1,* 18-164.

Featherman, D. L. (1983). Life-span perspectives in social science research. In P. B. Baltes & O. G. Brim, Jr. (Eds.), *Life-span development and behavior* (Vol. 5, pp. 1-57). New York: Academic Press.

Featherman, D. L., & Lerner, R. M. (1985). Ontogenesis and sociogenesis: Problematics for theory about development across the lifespan. *American Sociological Review, 50,* 659-676.

Featherman, D. L., Spenner, K. I., & Tsunematsu, N. (1988). Class and the socialization of children: Constancy, change, or irrelevance? In R. M. Lerner, E. M. Hetherington, & M. Perlmutter (Eds.), *Child development in life-span perspective* (pp. 67-90). Hillsdale, NJ: Lawrence Erlbaum.

Feldman, M. W., & Lewontin, R. C. (1975). The heritability hang-up. *Science, 190,* 1163-1168.

Finkelstein, J. W. (1993). Familial influences on adolescent health. In R. M. Lerner (Ed.), *Early adolescence: Perspectives on research, policy, and intervention* (pp. 111-126). Hillsdale, NJ: Lawrence Erlbaum.

Fisher, C. B., & Brennan, M. (1992). Application and ethics in developmental psychology. In D. L. Featherman, R. M. Lerner, & M. Perlmutter (Eds.), *Life-span development and behavior* (Vol. 11, pp. 189-219). Hillsdale, NJ: Lawrence Erlbaum.

Fisher, C. B., & Lerner, R. M. (1994). Foundations of applied developmental psychology. In C. B. Fisher & R. M. Lerner (Eds.), *Applied developmental psychology* (pp. 3-20). New York: McGraw-Hill.

Fisher, C. B., Murray, J. P., Dill, J. R., Hagen, J. W., Hogan, M. J., Lerner, R. M., Rebok, G. W., Sigel, I., Sostek, A. M., Smyer, M. A., Spencer, M. B., & Wilcox, B. (1993). The national conference on graduate education in the applications of developmental science across the life span. *Journal of Applied Developmental Psychology, 14,* 1-10.

Fisher, C. B., & Tryon, W. W. (1990). Emerging ethical issues in an emerging field. In C. B. Fisher & W. W. Tryon (Eds.), *Ethics in applied developmental psychology: Emerging issues in an emerging field*. Norwood, NJ: Ablex.

Ford, D. L., & Lerner, R. M. (1992). *Developmental systems theory: An integrative approach*. Newbury Park, CA: Sage.

Forsythe, P. W. (1991, November). *Beyond cooperation: Family preservation services as a catalyst for working together*. Paper presented at the Creating Caring Communities Conference, Michigan State University, East Lansing.

Freud, A. (1969). Adolescence as a developmental disturbance. In G. Caplan & S. Lebovier (Eds.), *Adolescence* (pp. 5-10). New York: Basic Books.

Garbarino, J. (1992). *Children and families in the social environment* (2nd ed.). Hawthorne, NY: Aldine.

Gottlieb, G. (1991). The experiential canalization of behavioral development: Theory. *Developmental Psychology, 27,* 4-13.

Gottlieb, G. (1992). *Individual development and evolution: The genesis of novel behavior*. New York: Oxford.

Gould, S. J. (1977). *Ontogeny and phylogeny*. Cambridge, MA: Belknap Press of Harvard.

Graham, S. (1992). "Most of the subjects were White and middle class": Trends in published research on African Americans in selected APA journals, 1970-1989. *American Psychologist, 5,* 629-639.

Guerney, L., & Arthur, J. (1984). Adolescent social relationships. In R. M. Lerner & N. L. Galambos (Eds.), *Experiencing adolescents: A sourcebook for parents, teachers, and teens*. New York: Garland.

Hackney, S. (1991). *Commencement address.* Philadelphia: University of Pennsylvania.

Hagen, J. W., Paul, B., Gibb, S., & Wolters, C. (1990, March). *Trends in research as reflected by publications in* Child Development: *1930-1989.* Paper presented at the biennial meeting of the Society for Research on Adolescence, Atlanta, GA.

Hahn, A. B. (1994). Toward a national youth development policy for young African-American males: The choices policymakers face. In R. B. Mincy (Ed.), *Nurturing young Black males: Challenges to agencies, programs, and social policy* (pp. 165-186). Washington, DC: The Urban Institute Press.

Hamburg, D. A. (1992). *Today's children: Creating a future for a generation in crisis.* New York: Times Books.

Harter, S. (1982). The Perceived Competence Scale for Children. *Child Development, 53,* 87-97.

Harter, S. (1983). *Supplementary description of the self-perception profile for child: Revision of the Perceived Competence Scale for Children.* Denver, CO: University of Denver Press.

Harter, S. (1988). Cause, correlates and the functional role of global self-worth: A life-span perspective. In J. Kolligian & R. J. Sternberg (Eds.), *Perceptions of competence and incompetence across the life-span.* New Haven, CT: Yale University Press.

Hebb, D. O. (1949). *The organization of behavior.* New York: Wiley.

Henry, W. (1990, April 9). Beyond the melting pot. *Time,* pp. 28-31.

Hernandez, D. J. (1993). *America's children: Resources from family, government, and the economy.* New York: Russell Sage Foundation.

Hetherington, E. M., & Baltes, P. B. (1988). Child psychology and life-span development. In E. M. Hetherington, R. M. Lerner, & M. Perlmutter (Eds.), *Child development in life-span perspective* (pp. 1-19). Hillsdale, NJ: Lawrence Erlbaum.

Hetherington, E. M., Lerner, R. M., & Perlmutter, M. (Eds.). (1988). *Child development in life-span perspective.* Hillsdale, NJ: Lawrence Erlbaum.

Hirsch, J. (1970). Behavior-genetic analysis and its biosocial consequences. *Seminars in Psychiatry, 2,* 89-105.

Hoffman, R. F. (1978). Developmental changes in human infant visual-evoked potentials to patterned stimuli recorded at different scalp locations. *Child Development, 49,* 110-118.

Hogan, R., Johnson, J. A., & Emler, N. P. (1978). A socioanalytic theory of moral development. *New Directions for Child Development, 2,* 1-18.

Howard, J. (1978). The influence of children's developmental dysfunction on marital quality and family interaction. In R. M. Lerner &. G. B. Spanier (Eds.), *Child influences on marital and family interaction: A life-span perspective* (pp. 275-298). New York: Academic Press.

Huston, A. C. (Ed.). (1992). *Children in poverty: Child development and public policy.* Cambridge, UK: Cambridge University Press.

Huston, A. C., McLoyd, V. C., & Coll, C. G. (1994). Children and poverty: Issues in contemporary research. *Child Development, 65,* 275-282.

Jacobs, F. H. (1988). The five-tiered approach to evaluation: Context and implementation. In H. Weiss & F. Jacobs (Eds.), *Evaluating family programs* (pp. 37-68). Hawthorne, NY: Aldine.

Jensen, L. (1988). Rural-urban differences in the utilization of ameliorative effects of welfare programs. *Policy Studies Review, 7,* 782-794.

Kahn, R. L., & Antonucci, T. C. (1980). Convoys over the life course: Attachment, roles, and social support. In P. B. Baltes & O. G. Brim, Jr. (Eds.), *Life-span development and behavior* (Vol. 3). Hillsdale, NJ: Lawrence Erlbaum.

Katchadourian, H. (1977). *The biology of adolescence.* San Francisco: Freeman.

Klerman, L. V. (1992). The health of poor children: Problems and programs. In A. C. Huston (Ed.), *Children in poverty: Child development and public policy* (pp. 1-22). Cambridge, UK: Cambridge University Press.

Kretzmann, J. P., & McKnight, J. L. (1993). *Building communities from the inside out: A path toward finding and mobilizing a community's assets* (Report). (Available from the Center for Urban Affairs and Policy Research, Northwestern University, 2040 Sheridan Road, Evanston, IL 60208)

Lanier, J. E. (1990). *Report to focus group colleagues on "Teaching," National Academy of Education Study on the Future of Educational Research.* Michigan State University, College of Education.

Lerner, J. V. (1994). *Working women and their families.* Thousand Oaks, CA: Sage.

Lerner, R. M. (1978). Nature, nurture, and dynamic interactionism. *Human Development, 21,* 1-20.

Lerner, R. M. (1979). A dynamic interactional concept of individual and social relationship development. In R. L. Burgess & T. L. Huston (Eds.), *Social exchange in developing relationships* (pp. 271-305). New York: Academic Press.

Lerner, R. M. (1982). Children and adolescents as producers of their own development. *Developmental Review, 2,* 342-370.

Lerner, R. M. (1984). *On the nature of human plasticity.* New York: Cambridge University Press.

Lerner, R. M. (1986). *Concepts and theories of human development* (2nd ed.). New York: Random House.

Lerner, R. M. (1988). Early adolescent transitions: The lore and the laws of adolescence. In M. D. Levine & E. R. McArarney (Eds.), *Early adolescent transitions* (pp. 1-40). Lexington, MA: D. C. Heath.

Lerner, R. M. (1991). Changing organism-context relations as the basic process of development: A developmental-contextual perspective. *Developmental Psychology, 27,* 27-32.

Lerner, R. M. (1992). *Final solutions: Biology, prejudice, and genocide.* University Park: Pennsylvania State University Press.

Lerner, R. M. (1993a). Investment in youth: The role of home economics in enhancing the life chances of America's children. *AHEA Monograph Series, 1,* 5-34.

Lerner, R. M. (1993b). Early adolescence: Toward an agenda for the integration of research, policy, and intervention. In R. M. Lerner (Ed.), *Early adolescence: Perspectives on research, policy, and intervention* (pp. 1-13). Hillsdale, NJ: Lawrence Erlbaum.

Lerner, R. M. (1994). Schools and adolescents. In P. C. McKenry & S. M. Gavazzi (Eds.), *Visions 2010: Families and adolescents* (Vol. 2[1], pp. 14-15, 42-43). Minneapolis, MN: National Council on Family Relations.

Lerner, R. M. (in press). Diversity and context in research, policy, and programs for children and adolescents: A developmental contextual perspective. In G. K. Brookins & M. B. Spencer (Eds.), *Ethnicity and diversity: Implications for research policies.* Hillsdale, NJ: Lawrence Erlbaum.

Lerner, R. M., & Busch-Rossnagel, N. A. (Eds.). (1981). *Individuals as producers of their development: A life-span perspective.* New York: Academic Press.

Lerner, R. M., & Fisher, C. B. (1994). From applied developmental psychology to applied developmental science: Community coalitions and collaborative careers. In C. B. Fisher & R. M. Lerner (Eds.), *Applied developmental psychology* (pp. 505-522). New York: McGraw-Hill.

Lerner, R. M., Hultsch, D. F., & Dixon, R. A. (1983). Contextualism and the character of developmental psychology in the 1970s. *Annals of the New York Academy of Sciences, 412,* 101-128.

Lerner, R. M., & Kauffman, M. B. (1985). The concept of development in contextualism. *Developmental Review, 5,* 309-333.

Lerner, R. M., & Lerner, J. V. (1983). Temperament-intelligence reciprocities in early childhood: A contextual model. In M. Lewis (Ed.), *Origins of intelligence: Infancy and early childhood.* New York: Plenum.

Lerner, R. M., & Lerner, J. V. (1987). Children in their contexts: A goodness of fit model. In J. B. Lancaster, J. Altmann, A. S. Rossi, & L. R. Sherrod (Eds.), *Parenting across the lifespan: Biosocial dimensions* (pp. 377-404). Chicago: Aldine.

Lerner, R. M., & Lerner, J. V. (1989). Organismic and social contextual bases of development: The sample case of early adolescence. In W. Damon (Ed.), *Child development today and tomorrow* (pp. 69-85). San Francisco: Jossey-Bass.

Lerner, R. M., & Miller, J. R. (1993). Integrating human development research and intervention for America's children: The Michigan State University model. *Journal of Applied Developmental Psychology, 14,* 347-364.

Lerner, R. M., Miller, J. R., Knott, J. H., Corey, K. E., Bynum, T. S., Hoopfer, L. C., McKinney, M. H., Abrams, L. A., Hula, R. C., & Terry, P. A. (1994). Integrating scholarship and outreach in human development research, policy, and service: A developmental perspective. In D. L. Featherman, R. M. Lerner, & M. Perlmutter (Eds.), *Life-span development and behavior* (Vol. 12, pp. 249-273). Hillsdale, NJ: Lawrence Erlbaum.

Lerner, R. M., Ostrom, C. W., & Freel, M. A. (in press). A developmental contextual perspective on health compromising and health enhancing behaviors. In J. Schulenberg, J. L. Maggs, & K. Hurrelmann (Eds.), *Health risks and developmental transitions during adolescence.* New York: Cambridge University Press.

Lerner, R. M., & Ryff, C. D. (1978). Implementation of the life-span view of human development: The sample case of attachment. In P. B. Baltes (Ed.), *Life-span development and behavior* (Vol. 1, pp. 1-44). New York: Academic Press.

Lerner, R. M., & Spanier, G. B. (Eds.). (1978). *Child influences on marital and family interaction: A life-span perspective.* New York: Academic Press.

Lerner, R. M., & Spanier, G. B. (1980). *Adolescent development: A life-span perspective.* New York: McGraw-Hill.

Lerner, R. M., Terry, P. A., McKinney, M. H., & Abrams, L. A. (1994). Addressing child poverty within the context of a community-collaborative university: Comments on Fabes, Martin, and Smith (1994) and McLoyd (1994). *Family and Consumer Sciences Research Journal, 23,* 67-75.

Lerner, R. M., & Tubman, J. (1989). Conceptual issues in studying continuity and discontinuity in personality development across life. *Journal of Personality, 57,* 343-373.

Levine, R. L., & Fitzgerald, H. E. (Eds.). (1992). *Analysis of dynamic psychological systems: Basic processes.* New York: Plenum.

Lewis, M., & Fiering, C. (1978). A child's social world. In R. M. Lerner & G. B. Spanier (Eds.), *Child influences on marital and family interaction* (pp. 47-66). New York: Academic Press.

Lewis, M., & Rosenblum, L. A. (Eds.). (1974). *The effect of the infant on its caregivers.* New York: Wiley.

Little, R. R. (1993, March). *What's working for today's youth: The issues, the programs, and the learnings.* Paper presented at an ICYF Fellows' Colloquium, Michigan State University, East Lansing.

Lynton, E. A., & Elman, S. E. (1987). *New priorities for the university: Meeting society's needs for applied knowledge and competent individuals.* San Francisco: Jossey-Bass.

MacDonald, M. (1994). *Reinventing systems: Collaborations to support families.* Cambridge, MA: Harvard Family Research Project.

Masters, R. D. (1978). Jean-Jacques is alive and well: Rousseau and contemporary sociobiology. *Daedalus, 107,* 93-105.

McKinney, M., Abrams, L. A., Terry, P. A., & Lerner, R. M. (1994). Child development research and the poor children of America: A call for a developmental contextual approach to research and outreach. *Family and Consumer Sciences Research Journal, 23,* 26-42.

McKnight, J. L., & Kretzmann, J. P. (1993). Mapping community capacity. *Michigan State University Community & Economic Development Program Community News,* pp. 1-4.

McLoyd, V. C. (1994). Research in the service of poor and ethnic/racial minority children: A moral imperative. *Family and Consumer Sciences Research Journal, 23,* 56-66.

McLoyd, V. C., & Wilson, L. (1992). The strain of living poor: Parenting, social support, and child mental health. In A. C. Huston (Ed.), *Children in poverty: Child development and public policy* (pp. 105-135). Cambridge, UK: Cambridge University Press.

Michigan State University Provost's Committee on University Outreach. (1993). *University outreach at Michigan State University: Extending knowledge to serve society.* East Lansing: Michigan State University.

Miller, J. R., & Lerner, R. M. (1994). Integrating research and outreach: Developmental contextualism and the human ecological perspective. *Home Economics Forum, 7,* 21-28.

Miller, P. B. (1993). *Building villages to raise our children: Evaluation.* Cambridge, MA: Harvard Family Research Project.

Mincy, R. B. (Ed.). (1994). *Nurturing young Black males: Challenges to agencies, programs, and social policy.* Washington, DC: The Urban Institute Press.

National Association of State Universities and Land-Grant Colleges. (1989). *State and land-grant universities: An American institution.* Washington, DC: Author.

National Council of Administrators of Home Economics Programs. (1991, October). *Creating a vision: The profession for the next century.* Report of the working conference. Pine Mountain, GA: Callaway Gardens.

National Research Council. (1993). *Losing generations: Adolescents in high-risk settings.* Washington, DC: National Academy Press.

Novikoff, A. B. (1945). The concept of integrative levels of biology. *Science, 62,* 209-215.

Obermiller, T. (1991). Investigations: A hard look at hard times. *University of Chicago Magazine, 84*(2), 34-38.

Ostrom, C. W., Lerner, R. M., & Freel, M. A. (1994). *Building the capacity of youth and families through university-community collaboration: The development-in-context evaluation (DICE) model.* (Available from the Institute for Children, Youth, and Families, Michigan State University, Suite 27 Kellogg Center, East Lansing, MI 48824)

Overton, W. F., & Reese, H. W. (1973). Models of development: Methodological implications. In J. R. Nesselroade & H. W. Reese (Eds.), *Life-span developmental psychology: Methodological issues* (pp. 65-86). New York: Academic Press.

Overton, W. F., & Reese, H. W. (1981). Conceptual prerequisites for an understanding of stability-change and continuity-discontinuity. *International Journal of Behavioral Development, 4,* 99-123.

Peirce, C. S. (1931). In C. Hartshorne, P. Weiss, & A. Burks (Eds.), *Collected papers of Charles Sanders Peirce* (Vol. 5, p. 86). Cambridge, MA: Harvard University Press.

Pepper, S. C. (1942). *World hypotheses.* Berkeley: University of California Press.

Piaget, J. (1950). *The psychology of intelligence.* New York: Harcourt Brace.

Piaget, J. (1972). Intellectual evolution from adolescence to adulthood. *Human Development, 15,* 1-12.

Pittman, K. J., & Zeldin, S. (1994). From deterrence to development: Shifting the focus of youth programs for African-American males. In R. B. Mincy (Ed.), *Nurturing young Black males: Challenges to agencies, programs, and social policy* (pp. 165-186). Washington, DC: The Urban Institute Press.

Reese, H. W., & Overton, W. F. (1970). Models of development and theories of development. In L. R. Goulet & P. B. Baltes (Eds.), *Life-span developmental psychology: Research and theory* (pp. 115-145). New York: Academic Press.

Riegel, K. F. (1975). Toward a dialectical theory of development. *Human Development, 18,* 50-64.

Riegel, K. F. (1976a). The dialectics of human development. *American Psychologist, 31,* 689-700.

Riegel, K. F. (1976b). From traits and equilibrium toward developmental dialectics. In W. J. Arnold & J. K. Cole (Eds.), *Nebraska symposium on motivation* (pp. 348-408). Lincoln: University of Nebraska Press.

Riley, M. W. (Ed.). (1979). *Aging from birth to death.* Washington, DC: American Association for the Advancement of Science.

Sahlins, M. D. (1978). The use and abuse of biology. In A. L. Caplan (Ed.), *The sociobiology debate.* New York: Harper & Row.

Sameroff, A. (1975). Transactional models in early social relations. *Human Development, 18,* 65-79.

Sameroff, A. J. (1983). Developmental systems: Contexts and evolution. In W. Kessen (Ed.), *Handbook of child psychology: Vol. 1. History, theory and methods* (pp. 237-294). New York: Wiley.

Schaie, K. W. (1965). A general model for the study of developmental problems. *Psychological Bulletin, 64,* 92-107.

Schaie, K. W. (1979). The primary mental abilities in adulthood: An exploration in the development of psychometric intelligence. In P. B. Baltes & O. G. Brim, Jr. (Eds.), *Life-span development and behavior* (Vol. 2, pp. 57-115). New York: Academic Press.

Schein, E. H. (1992). *Organizational culture and leadership.* San Francisco: Jossey-Bass.

Schneirla, T. C. (1957). The concept of development in comparative psychology. In D. B. Harris (Ed.), *The concept of development* (pp. 78-108). Minneapolis: University of Minnesota Press.

Schorr, L. B. (1988). *Within our reach: Breaking the cycle of disadvantage.* New York: Doubleday.

Schorr, L. B. (1992). Effective programs for children growing up in concentrated poverty. In A. C. Huston (Ed.), *Children in poverty: Child development and public policy* (pp. 260-281). Cambridge, UK: Cambridge University Press.

Senge, P. M. (1990). *The fifth discipline: The art and practice of the learning organization.* New York: Doubleday.

Simmons, R. G., & Blyth, D. A. (1987). *Moving into adolescence: The impact of pubertal change and school context.* Hawthorne, NY: Aldine.

Simons, J. M., Finlay, B., & Yang, A. (1991). *The adolescent and young adult fact book.* Washington, DC: Children's Defense Fund.

Slavin, R., Karweit, N., & Wasik, B. (1994). *Preventing early school failure: Research on effective strategies.* Boston, MA: Allyn & Bacon.

Steinberg, L. (1983). The varieties and effects of work during adolescence. In M. Lamb, A. Brown, & B. Rogoff (Eds.), *Advances in developmental psychology* (Vol. 3, pp. 1-37). Hillsdale, NJ: Lawrence Erlbaum.

Thomas, A., & Chess, S. (1977). *Temperament and development.* New York: Brunner/Mazel.

Thomas, A., & Chess, S. (1980). *The dynamics of psychological development.* New York: Brunner/Mazel.

Thomas, A., & Chess, S. (1981). The role of temperament in the contributions of individuals to their development. In R. M. Lerner & N. A. Busch-Rossnagel (Eds.), *Individuals as producers of their own development: A life-span perspective.* New York: Academic Press.

Thomas, A., Chess, S., Birch, H. G., Hertzig, M. E., & Korn, S. (1963). *Behavioral individuality in early childhood.* New York: New York University Press.

Tobach, E. (1981). Evolutionary aspects of the activity of the organism and its development. In R. M. Lerner & N. A. Busch-Rossnagel (Eds.), *Individuals as producers of their development: A life-span perspective* (pp. 37-68). New York: Academic Press.

Tobach, E., & Greenberg, G. (1984). The significance of T. C. Schneirla's contribution to the concept of levels of integration. In G. Greenberg & E. Tobach (Eds.), *Behavioral evolution and integrative levels* (pp. 1-7). Hillsdale, NJ: Lawrence Erlbaum.

Tobach, E., & Schneirla, T. C. (1968). The biopsychology of social behavior of animals. In R. E. Cooke & S. Levin (Eds.), *Biologic basis of pediatric practice* (pp. 68-82). New York: McGraw-Hill.

Tubman, J. G., & Lerner, R. M. (1994). Stability of affective experiences of parents and their children from adolescence to young adulthood. *Journal of Adolescence, 17,* 81-98.

U.S. Bureau of the Census. (1991, August). *The Hispanic population in the United States: March, 1991* (Current Population Reports, Series P-20, No. 455). Washington, DC: U.S. Government Printing Office.

U.S. Department of Commerce. (1991, August). *Poverty in the United States: 1990.* Washington, DC: Author.

Usdan, M. (1994, January). The relationship between school boards and general purpose government. *Phi Delta Kappan,* pp. 374-377.

Villarruel, F. A., & Lerner, R. M. (Eds.). (1994). Promoting community-based programs for socialization and learning. In *New directions for child development* (Vol. 63). San Francisco: Jossey-Bass.

von Eye, A. (1990a). *Introduction to configural frequency analysis: The search for types and antitypes in cross-classifications.* Cambridge, UK: Cambridge University Press.

von Eye, A. (Ed.). (1990b). *Statistical methods in longitudinal research: Principles and structuring change.* New York: Academic Press.

von Eye, A. (Ed.). (1990c). *Statistical methods in longitudinal research: Time series and categorical longitudinal data.* New York: Academic Press.

Vondracek, F. W., Lerner, R. M., & Schulenberg, J. E. (1983). The concept of development in vocational theory and intervention. *Journal of Vocational Behavior, 23,* 179-202.

Vondracek, F. W., Lerner, R. M., & Schulenberg, J. E. (1986). *Career development: A life-span developmental approach.* Hillsdale, NJ: Lawrence Erlbaum.

Votruba, J. C. (1992). Promoting the extension of knowledge in service to society. *Metropolitan Universities, 3*(3), 72-80.

Washburn, S. L. (Ed.). (1961). *Social life of early men.* New York: Wenner-Gren Foundation for Anthropological Research.

Washington, V. (1992, September). *Leadership for children in the 21st century: Professors, public policy, and philanthropy.* Paper presented at the ICYF Fellows Colloquium, Michigan State University, East Lansing.

Wehlage, G., Rutter, R., Smith, G., Lesko, N., & Fernandez, R. (1989). *Reducing the risk: Schools as communities of support.* New York: Falmer.

Weiss, H. B. (1987a). Family support and education in early childhood programs. In S. Kagan, D. Powell, B. Weissbourd, & E. Zigler (Eds.), *America's family support programs* (pp. 133-160). New Haven, CT: Yale University Press.

Weiss, H. B. (1987b). Evaluating social programs: What have we learned? *Society, 25*(1), 40-45.

Weiss, H. B., & Greene, J. C. (1992). An empowerment partnership for family support and education programs and evaluations. *Family Science Review, 5*, 131-148.

Weiss, H. B., & Hite, S. (1986). Evaluation: Who's doing it and how? A report from a national program survey conducted by the Harvard Family Research Project. *Family Resource Coalition Report,* No. 3, pp. 4-7.

Weiss, H. B., & Jacobs, F. (Eds.). (1988). *Evaluating family programs.* Hawthorne, NY: Aldine.

Werner, H. (1957). The concept of development from a comparative and organismic point of view. In D. B. Harris (Ed.), *The concept of development* (pp. 125-148). Minneapolis: University of Minnesota Press.

Wetzel, J. (1987). *American youth: A statistical snapshot.* New York: William T. Grant Foundation.

Wilson, W. J. (1987). *The truly disadvantaged: The inner city, the underclass, and public policy.* Chicago: University of Chicago Press.

Name Index

Abbett, W. S., xxi
Abood, C., xxi
Abrams, L. A., xx, 1, 100
Ahlburg, D. A., 40
Allen, V., xxi
Allison, K. W., 40, 70
Alvarez, B., 93, 97
Ames, C., xxi, 93
Ames, R., 93
Anastasi, A., 18
Anderton, J. F., Jr., xxi
Andrews, M. L., xx
Anthony, V. D., xxi
Antonucci, T. C., 123
Arthur, J., 124
Asmussen, J., xx

Baca Zinn, M., 24
Baltes, M. M., 10, 24, 34, 59, 79
Baltes, P. B., xxiv, 20, 30, 124
Barckholtz, P., xxi
Barnard, K. E., xxiii
Barnes, C. L., xx
Barringer, F., 39
Bell, R. Q., 17
Belsky, J., 24, 26
Benavides, A., xxi
Berning, R. G., xxi

Bettinghaus, E. P., xxi
Binsfeld, C., xxi
Birch, H. G., 17
Birkel, R., xxiv, 126
Block, J., 10
Blyth, D. A., 124
Bond, J. T., xx
Bonnen, J. T., 102
Bornstein, M. H., xxiv, 25
Bowman, B., xxi
Boyer, E. L., xvi, xxiv, 13, 101, 103, 106,
    109, 126, 127
Brazelton, T. B., 20, 21
Brennan, M., 12, 36
Brickman, J. A., xx, xxi
Brim, O. G., Jr., xxiv, 15, 20
Bronfenbrenner, U., xxiv, 14, 15, 23, 24, 26,
    27, 28, 48, 52-53, 89
Brookins, G., xxiv
Brooks-Gunn, J., xxiii, xxiv
Brown, N. A., xxi
Bubolz, M., 103
Busch-Rossnagel, N. A., xxiv, 22, 126
Butler, E. P., xxiii
Bynum, T. S., xx

Carnegie Corporation of New York, 2, 7, 8,
    40, 46, 62, 63, 64, 65, 74, 120

Carnegie Council on Adolescent Development, 2, 61, 92
Castellino, D., xx
Center for the Study of Social Policy, 7, 9, 10, 11
Chacon, A. R., xx
Chapel, L. K., xx
Chess, S., xxiv, 16, 17, 18, 20, 23, 124
Children's Defense Fund, 8
Church, R. L., xx
Colby, A., xxiv
Colliar, A., xxi
Cook, D., xxi
Corey, K. E., xx, xxi
Cornell, G., xx
Cronbach, L., 81, 86
Crouter, A. C., 26
Curtin, S. C., xx

Damon, W., xxiv
Darden, J. T., xxi
Davis, H., xx
Davis, M., xx
De Vita, C. J., 40
Dearing, J., xx
DiBiaggio, J., xxiv
Dickson, W. P., xx
Dilley, E., xxi
Dittmann-Kohli, F., 35
Dixon, R. A., xxiv, 14, 16, 35, 85
Dowling, C. C., xx
Dryfoos, J. G., xiv, xviii, xxiv, xxv, 1, 2, 11, 39, 56, 60, 62, 65, 66, 68, 69, 70, 71, 73, 74, 76, 77, 78, 80, 84, 85, 91, 92, 93-96, 97, 98, 100, 111, 113, 117, 120, 122
Duncan, G. J., 8
Dye, J., xx

East, P. L., xxiv
Eccles, J. S., 93
Edelman, M. W., xiv, xxiv, 113, 128
Eitzen, D. S., 24
Elder, G. H., Jr., xxiv, 20, 23, 30, 48
Elman, S. E., 13
Emler, N. P., 16
Enarson, H. L., 13, 101

Entwisle, D., xxiv
Erikson, E., 124

Fear, F. A., xx
Featherman, D. L., xxiii, xxiv, 13, 16, 20, 40, 41
Fedewa, C., xxi
Feldman, M. W., 18
Ferguson, J., xxi
Fiering, C., 24
Finkelstein, J. W., 28
Finlay, B., 2
Fisher, C. B., xxiv, 12, 36, 56, 57, 58-59, 100, 104, 122, 126
Fitzgerald, H. E., xx, 107
Ford, D. H., xxiv, 14, 28, 77, 79, 89, 103, 122
Forsythe, P. W., 55
Freel, M. A., xx, 81
Freud, A., 124

Galambos, N., xxiv
Gerber, C., xxii
Garcia Coll, C., 1
Gibb, S., 12
Gonzales, D., xxii
Gonzales, W. G., xxii
Gottlieb, G. J., xxiv, 27
Gould, S. J., 16
Graham, S., 12, 38
Greenberg, G., xxiv, 15, 30
Greene, J. C., 81, 82, 83-84, 85, 86, 87, 89, 90, 91, 125
Griffore, R. J., xx
Guerney, L., 124

Hackney, S., 106
Hagen, J. W., xxiv, 12, 36, 37, 48
Hahn, A. B., 119
Hamburg, B. A., xxiv
Hamburg, D. A., xiii, xiv, xviii, xxiv, 1, 2, 6, 8, 10, 11, 42, 43-44, 45, 46-47, 60, 62, 65, 66, 68, 69, 70, 71, 74, 75, 79, 80, 111, 113, 118-119, 120, 121
Harrison, M. G., xxii
Harter, S., 64
Hauser, S. T., xxiv

Haveman, J. K., xxii
Hebb, D. O., 78
Hekman, R., xxii
Henry, W., 39
Hernandez, D. J., xxiv, 2, 10, 30, 40, 41-42,
    43, 44, 47-48, 45, 46, 47, 48, 62, 93
Hertzig, M. E., 17
Hesterman, O., xx
Hetherington, E. M., xxiv, 20, 59
Hirsch, J., 18
Hite, S., 82
Hoffman, R. F., 16
Hogan, R., 16
Hollister, D., xxii
Holman, C., xxii
Hoopfer, L. C., xx
Howard, J., 28
Huberman, M., xxiii
Hula, R. C., xx
Hultsch, D. F., xxiv, 14, 16
Huston, A. C., 1, 7, 8, 9, 93, 100, 117, 119

Ilgen, D., xx
Imig, G. L., xx, xxi
Ivory, R., xxii

Jacobs, F. H., xxiv, 81, 83, 85, 86, 91
Jensen, L., 7
Johnson, J. A., 16

Kaagan, S., xx
Kagen, J., xxiv
Kahn, R. L., 123
Kallen, D. J., xx
Katchadourian, H., 124
Kauffman, M. B., 13, 16
Keilitz, G., xxii
Keith, J. G., xx
Kissman, K. L., xxii
Klerman, L. V., 8
Klomparens, K., xx
Knott, J. H., xx
Kopp, C. B., xxiv
Korn, S. J., xxiv, 17
Koslowski, B., 20
Kostelnik, M. J., xx

Kreppner, K., xxiv
Kretzmann, J. P., 48, 49, 83, 86, 87, 97
Kuhn, D., xxiv

Lamb, M. E., xxiii, xxiv
Lanier, J. E., 35-36, 52
Lenerz, K., xxiv
Lerner, J. V., xx, xxiv, 23, 25, 44, 124
Lerner, J. S., xxv
Lerner, R. M., 1, 6, 11, 12, 13, 14, 15, 16, 17,
    18, 20, 22, 23, 24, 25, 27, 28, 30, 32,
    34, 35, 37, 38, 51, 55, 56, 58-59, 63,
    70, 77, 78, 79, 80, 81, 84, 85, 89, 93,
    100, 101, 103, 104, 111, 112, 113,
    121, 122, 123, 124, 125, 126, 127
Levine, R. L., 107
Lewis, M., xxiv, 17, 20, 24
Lewontin, R. C., 18
Lipsitt, L. P., 34
Lindsay, J., xxii
Little, R. R., xiv, xxii, xxiv, 66, 67, 68, 69,
    70, 72, 73, 74, 80, 81, 113, 115, 122-
    123
Liu, H., xxii
Lynton, E. A., 13

MacDonald, M., 82
Magnusson, D., xxiii
Main, M., 20
Mark, C., xxii
Marshall, A., xxii
Massie, D., xxii
Masters, R. D., 16
Mawby, R. G., xxii
Mawdsley, J. K., xxii
McAdoo, H. P., xx
McAdoo, J. L., xx
McConaughy, P., xxii
McDonald, J., xxii
McKinney, M. H., xx, 1, 12, 100, 101
McKnight, J. L., xxiv, 48, 49, 83, 86, 87, 97
McLoyd, V. C., xxiv, 1, 8, 12, 38, 39, 94, 127
McPherson, M. P., xxiv
Metzler, J., xx
Meyer, L., xxii
Michigan State University Provost's Commit-
    tee on University Outreach, 12, 104

Midgley, C., 93
Miller, G. H., xxii
Miller, J. R., xx, xxi, 11, 12, 13, 30, 51, 58,
     101, 103, 111, 112, 121
Miller, P. B., 62, 82, 91
Mincy, R. B., 2, 63
Modell, J., 30
Molidor, J. B., xx
Moore, J. S., xxii
Murphy, M., xxii
Mussen, P. H., xxiv

National Association of State Universities
     and Land-Grant Colleges, 101, 102
National Council of Administrators of
     Home Economics Programs, 13
National Research Council, 2, 120, 121
Novikoff, A. B., 15

O'Laughlin, C. M., xxii
Obermiller, T., 55
Ostrom, C. W., xx, 81, 84, 85, 125
Overton, W. F., xxiv, 16
Owens, D., xxii

Pacynski, B., xxii
Palmer, E. L., xxiii
Parks, J. F., xx
Paterson, D. M., xxii
Paul, B., 12
Pepper, S. C., 23
Perkins, D. F., xx
Perlmutter, M., xxiv, 59
Peterson, P., xx
Peterson, R. E., xxii
Piaget, J., 123
Pierre, P. A., xxi
Pittman, K. J., xxiii, xxiv, 115, 119, 120, 121
Pollack, L., xxii
Pollard, J., xxii
Poston, F. L., xxi
Randall, W. L., xxii
Ray, J., xxii
Reed, C. S., xx
Reese, H. W., xxiv, 16, 34
Revzin, A., xxi

Reynolds, D., xxii
Reynolds, N., xxii
Richards, E. S., 103
Riegel, K. F., 16
Riley, M. W., 20
Rios de Betancourt, E., xxii
Rivera, O., xxii
Roberts, K., xxii
Roberts Mason, B., xxii
Robinson, T. C., xxiii
Roman, L. A. W., xx
Rosenblum, L. A., 17, 20, 23
Rothert, M., xxi
Rutledge, T., xxiii, 16, 18, 20
Ryff, C. D., 35, 80

Sahlins, M. D., 16
Sameroff, A. J., xxiv, 16
Sandmann, L., xx
Sauer, R. J., xix, xxiii, xxv
Sawyer-Koch, B. J., xxiii
Schadewald, S., xxiii
Schaie, K. W., xxiv, 20, 124
Schein, E. H., 106
Schiamberg, L. B., xx
Schneirla, T. C., xxiv, 16, 17, 20, 63, 78
Schorr, L. B., xiv, xviii, xxiv, 1, 6, 8, 11, 56,
     60, 62, 65, 66, 67, 68, 69, 71, 73, 74,
     75, 76, 78, 93, 94, 111, 113, 117, 120,
     122
Schrock, K., xxiii
Schulenberg, J. E., xxiv, 20
Scott, D. K., xxiv
Scott-Jones, D., xxiv
Seefeldt, V., xx
Senge, P. M., 107
Shebuski, D., xxiii
Sheehan, P., xxiii
Sherrod, L. R., xxiv
Shingleton, J. D., xxiii
Silbereisen, R. K., xxiii
Simmons, R. G., 124
Simon, L. A. K., xxiv
Simons, J. M., 2, 7, 9, 10, 11
Smith, J., 35
Smith, L. W., xxiii
Smyer, M. A., 126
Sontag, M. S., 103

Spanier, G. B., xxiii, xxiv, 17, 20, 24, 63, 123
Sparks, H., xx
Spence, L., xx
Spencer, M. B., xxiv
Spenner, K. I., 40
Stabenow, D., xxiii
Stanford, L., xx
Staudinger, U. M., 35
Steinberg, L., 71
Stephens, C., xx
Stovall, B., xxiii
Sullivan, J. M., xxiii

Tableman, B., xxiii
Takanishi, R., xxv
Tamis-LeMonda, C. S., 25
Taylor, C. S., xx
Terry, P. A., xx, 1, 100
Thomas, A., xxv, 17, 23
Thompson, C., xx
Tiedje, J., xx
Tiedje, L. B., xx
Tobach, E., xxv, 15, 16, 27, 30, 63
Traxler, B., xxiii
Tryon, W. W., 59
Tsunematsu, N., 40
Tubman, J., xxv, 28, 124

U.S. Bureau of the Census, 7
U.S. Department of Commerce, 10, 43

Valentine, N. L., xix
Villarruel, F. A., xx, 63
von Eye, A., 60

Vondracek, F. W., xxv, 20
Votruba, J. C., xx, xxi, 126, 127

Walker, W., xxiii
Wapner, S., xxv
Washburn, S. L., 16
Washington, V., xxv, 112, 113
Weill, W. B., xx
Weiss, H. B., 81, 82, 83-84, 85, 86, 87, 89,
   90, 91, 125
Weiss, R. E., xxiii
Werbelow, J., xxiii
Werner, H., 30
Wetzel, J., 39
Wheeler, W., xix
White, S. H., xxv
Williams, H. S., xxiii
Williams, W., xxiii
Willis, S., xxv
Wilson, B. E., xx
Wilson, L., 8, 94
Wilson, W. J., 1, 55
Windle, M., xxv
Wolters, C., 12
Wood, D. L., xxi
Wotring, J., xxiii
Wright, T. D., xxiii

Yang, A., 2

Zeldin, S., 115, 119, 120, 121

Zucker, R. A., xxv

Subject Index

Applied developmental science (ADS), 12, 56, 104, 122
  ethical issues for, 59
  principles of, 58
Asset mapping, 87

Carnegie Corporation of New York, 2, 45, 62, 63, 64-65
Carnegie Council on Adolescent Development, 2, 61, 92
Center for the Study of Social Policy, xxiv, 2
Chicago Urban Poverty and Family Life Project, 55
Child and youth poverty, 6, 7-10, 47-48
  across age groups, 8
  across geographic regions, 7
  across racial or ethnic groups, 7-8
  maternal risk factors associated with, 9-10
Child effects, 17, 18, 21, 23
Child poverty. See Child and youth poverty
Children's Defense Fund, xxiv, 2

Developmental contextualism, 13, 124, 125
  and human development, 33-60
  and program design and evaluation, 92

and research, 101
circular function model of, 21-22
definition of, xvii
goodness-of-fit model of, 22-23
overview of, 14-32
See also Outreach scholarship, developmental contextual approach to; Policy, national youth, implications of developmental contextualism for
Developmental system, preventive interventions in, 78-80
Development-in-context evaluation (DICE), 125
  features of, 87-91
  guides for, 85-86
  model of, 84-85
Diversity
  of children, 36-40
  of poor communities, 48-51
  of the American family, 40-48

Evaluation methods, collaborative, 81-87

Family, *Ozzie-and-Harriet*, 40, 46
4-H programs, 62

Girl Scouts of the USA, 62
Goodness of fit, 16, 124
    See also Developmental contextualism,
        goodness-of-fit model of

Harvard Family Research Project, 83
Hatch Act (1887), 102
Home oekology, 103
Human development
    Bronfenbrenner's model of the ecology
        of, 26-27
    descriptive research in, 33
    diversity in, 38-40 *See also* Diversity
    explanatory research in, 33, 34, 35
    integrated agenda for, 54-56
    policies and programs in, 51-52, 54

International Youth Foundation (IYF), 66,
    68, 70, 72, 74, 123
Interventionist inquiry, 35

Michigan State University Provost's Com-
    mittee on University Outreach, 104
Morrill Act (1862), 101
Morrill Act (1890), 102

National Association of State Universities
    and Land-Grant Colleges, 101
National Research Council, 2, 121
National Task Force on Applied Develop-
    mental Science, 57-58

Outreach scholarship, 12, 104-115

and community collaboration, 110-
    115
campus context of, 105-110
developmental contextual approach to,
    107-109

Panel Study on Income Dynamics, 8
Parallel processing, 15
Plasticity, 34, 35
Policy, national youth, 118
    and academic policy change, 126-127
    implications of developmental contextu-
        alism for, 122-125

Reductionism, 15
Risk behaviors, adolescent
    temporal trends in, 6
    types of, 2-6

Schools, failure of, 93
Schools, full-service, 94-96
    components of, 97-98
Smith-Lever Act (1914), 102

University, land-grant, 101-103

YMCA, 62
Youth development
    crisis of, 11
    qualities of, 61-62
Youth programs, successful, 65-76
features of, 68-76

About the Author

Richard M. Lerner is Professor of Family and Child Ecology, Psychology, Pediatrics and Human Development, and Counseling, Educational Psychology, and Special Education. He is the Director of the Institute for Children, Youth, and Families at Michigan State University. A developmental psychologist, he received a Ph.D. in 1971 from the City University of New York. He has been a fellow at the Center for Advanced Study in the Behavioral Sciences and is a fellow of the American Association for the Advancement of Science, the American Psychological Association, the American Psychological Society, and the American Association of Applied and Preventive Psychology. The author or editor of 30 books and more than 200 scholarly articles and chapters, he is known for his theory of and research about relations between human development and contextual or ecological change. He is the founding editor of the *Journal of Research on Adolescence*.